TOM KERRIDGE

Outdoor Cooking

TOM KERRIDGE

Outdoor Cooking

THE ULTIMATE MODERN BARBECUE BIBLE

BLOOMSBURY ABSOLUTE

LONDON · OXFORD · NEW YORK · NEW DELHI · SYDNEY

TO BEF AND ACEY
WANNA START A FIRE?!

Contents

LET'S GET FIRED UP

Nothing says summertime like getting family or a few mates over, lighting up the barbecue and cooking up a feast. Cooking outside, whether you're on the beach, around a campfire or just in your back garden, is all about having fun and creating memories. It's a relaxed way of cooking and eating, and I love it. But just because it's laid-back, it doesn't mean it can't be special. Barbecues have come a long way since a couple of burnt sausages and a packet of frozen burgers! I'm going to share some of my favourite meals for cooking over flames and hot coals with you, and I'll show you how to introduce loads of amazing flavour through fire and smoke.

Cooking over direct heat is a really fresh way to eat and a true celebration of ingredients. It's about pairing meat, fish and veg with some key flavourings, and then letting the barbecue work its magic. One of the things I love most is that it's a different process every time – it's not like turning on the oven and walking away. As a chef, I'm used to being surrounded by high-tech equipment in my kitchen and everything being very exact and precise, but cooking outside allows me to get back in touch with my instincts – it's just me and the flames. You soon get to know how things will look and feel when

they're ready, and how hot the coals need to be. It's all about watching and checking, rather than strict timings. It doesn't have to be perfect. And don't worry if there are some little extra charred bits: they always add to the flavour!

IT'S NOT ALL ABOUT BURGERS

Although sometimes it kind of is! Who doesn't love a juicy burger, freshly cooked on a barbie? There's nothing like layering it up with all your favourite condiments, maybe a cheese slice or two (I won't tell anyone) and topping with a few crunchy, vinegary pickles. It's pretty hard to eat a burger politely, and that's another thing I love about barbecues. They're not the place to wear your best white t-shirt!

I can smell barbecue smoke from several gardens away – it's like the scent of summer to me and it makes me want to get straight out there and fire up the grill. Getting everyone together and serving up some great food, not much beats that feeling as day turns to evening and the heat of the sun dips – it's the ideal time to put something else on the barbecue (maybe a pudding) to keep the day going on longer.

A barbecue isn't like a regular meal indoors where you have just one plate of food.

You can keep coming back for more, piling that plate high with all those amazing flavours. Rules don't apply when it comes to cooking outside – it's like one big long buffet. There's nothing to stop you having Japanese pork skewers next to Spanish-inspired seafood, next to a ketchup-covered hot dog. It will all be delicious and it's the perfect opportunity to try something new.

I've been really lucky to have eaten in some awesome places around the world, but it's not always to do with how fancy the location or food is. One of the best meals I've ever had was some street food in Singapore. It was around 3 a.m. after a long shift working in the kitchen, and we sat on plastic chairs eating sticky grilled aubergine. It was so simple, but packed with flavour. But that meal wasn't just about the food. Much of the experience came from the atmosphere and the other people there. Another time, we ate at a tiny taco hut in Tucson, 50 miles from the Mexican border. The flavours coming out of that shack, where they were cooking over coals and charred wood, were unbelievable. You just can't replicate that kind of environment. Closer to home, I have so many lovely memories of cooking on the beach in Cornwall – portable barbecue in the back of the car, drinks in a cooler, just hanging out with friends and family and enjoying time together.

I reckon when most people think of barbecues, it's going to be meat of some kind that comes to mind – whether that's a burger, sausages, a steak or some chicken wings. But there is also

a whole world of other ingredients to try and the recipes in this book will show you some amazing ways with seafood and veg too.

Whatever you choose, if you're going to the trouble of getting coals in, lighting a barbecue and standing there while you're cooking, then it's definitely worth making sure you're using some good-quality ingredients and taking a moment to consider how particular cuts of meat, or different fish or veg, might respond to flame-cooking. It doesn't have to be expensive, but there are a few things that will make a big difference when grilling over direct heat. For example, meat with a higher fat content will stay nice and juicy, and chunky fish will be less likely to stick to your barbecue. You can read more on how to get the most from your ingredients at the start of each chapter.

ADDING FLAVOUR

Cooking outside is all about the flavourings that you add before you start. We have been cooking over fire since we were cavemen dragging a woolly mammoth back to camp, so pretty much every country in the world has developed their own techniques and ways of adding flavour. I think all of them bring something special and unique.

It's no surprise that I love a bit of spice and heat in my food, and cooking over flames lends itself to trying out some bold flavours. Korean barbecue has become really popular here in recent years, and they aren't shy with their chillies in Korea. They use a fermented chilli paste called gochujang, which adds an amazing smoky heat – I've used it in my take on Korean barbecue on page 76. Then there's the more subtle approach to aromatics from across the Middle East, which brings gentle warmth to your cooking; you can taste it in the chicken shawarma on page 55. Indian cooking can be an inspiration for barbecues too, as lots of Indian dishes are cooked on a tandoor, which is very similar. Check out the spiced monkfish on page 114 for a feast full of fresh and punchy Indian flavours, or the tandoori fish skewers on page 122.

The Deep South of the USA is arguably the most famous for its barbecue tradition. For the pit masters there, it's not just a way of cooking, but a way of life. The kind of barbecue they really excel at is long slow cooking, which allows all those deep, rich, smoky flavours to develop over time. You'll taste this in the baby back ribs on page 85. You really can go on a round-the-world trip from your back garden!

What influences and unites all of these is the way they introduce flavour. The two main ways to add flavour before cooking over fire are through marinades (which can also help tenderise your meat before cooking and help stop everything from drying out) and dry rubs (which are spice blends that form a coating over your ingredients and then go on to create an amazing spiced crust). Both of these allow

the flavours to permeate right through the food for maximum impact. A third way to add even more taste and texture is through a glaze. A glaze is brushed on during cooking to provide an extra layer of caramelised flavour and that finger-licking barbecue stickiness we all love. If your marinade contains sweet ingredients, then it can often double up as a glaze – just brush any leftover marinade directly onto your meat, fish or veg as it cooks.

When it comes to getting the combination of barbecue flavours just right, you're aiming for a balance of sweet, salt, heat and acidity. Cooking over flames always brings a lovely bitter-sweet caramelisation, and you can add extra sweetness through grilled fruit, such as peaches, pineapple and nectarines (see pages 24, 218 and 224). These hold their shape on a barbecue and take on a buttery depth of flavour as they cook. Marinades and dry rubs often have sweetness too, with ingredients like brown sugar, honey, maple syrup or even apple juice. And failing all that, ketchup will provide a good dollop of sweetness! There's nothing wrong with picking up a bottle of it at the supermarket, but if you have a bit of time then the recipe on page 68 will add a whole other dimension to your barbecue.

That sweetness needs to be balanced by some acidity to cut through it. Acidity can come from something as simple as a squeeze of lemon juice or a grating of lime or lemon zest, or it can be in the form of vinegar in a dressing or marinade. It's what elevates a dish and brings it a freshness, helping all those great flavours burst into life.

When it comes to heat, that's partly down to personal preference – and whether you've got kids eating with you. Just bear in mind that robust meat like pork, beef and lamb can take more spice than delicate fish and shellfish, where you're going to want a gentler touch. You can always keep a bottle of hot sauce to hand for those who want to up the fiery heat!

But, of course, the one thing that's unique to cooking outdoors is smoke. You really can't recreate that inside and it's what makes this way of preparing food so exciting and special – and a bit unpredictable. The subtle layers of flavour that smoke brings to even simple pieces of fish or grilled veggies is just amazing.

If you want to take it to the next level and become a bit of a barbecue aficionado, you can experiment with adding even more flavour to the smoke by introducing wood chips to your hot coals. You can get really obsessed with the different effects these will have on the food – cherry wood versus maple wood or apple wood, for example, will all give subtle variations in the smoky taste they give out.

A simpler way to introduce extra flavour is to throw some woody herbs like rosemary, thyme or bay directly onto the hot coals while you're cooking. Both approaches will introduce some amazing aromatics to your barbecue.

ENJOY THE PROCESS

I really enjoy the whole process of barbecuing. I love saying, 'right, on Sunday we're going to cook outside', then spending time planning the menu, getting the coals together and preparing the food ahead. It's not like turning on the oven a little while before you want to eat – it's a much more tactile process from start to finish. If I'm cooking for other people then I want to make it really special and turn the barbecue into a bit of an event. Outdoor cooking is also great for getting the kids involved: they can help you with the prep and, as long as you keep a close eye on them near that intense heat, they can help you by flipping a burger or turning over a skewer. It's a brilliant way to teach them about cooking, food and flavours.

Sometimes, though, I know you just want to light the coals and cook something quickly, and it really doesn't need to be more elaborate than a basic barbie with a couple of juicy sausages. The important thing is that you enjoy it. Barbecues are perfect for cooking up a load of food, piling it up high and getting everyone involved. When you want to eat pretty quickly, it's all about the prep you do beforehand – marinating and getting sauces and sides ready so you're good to go when everyone's arrived. There are plenty of easy recipes in the following chapters you can prepare ahead and cook quickly, meaning you can spend more time doing what really matters: kicking back and making memories.

My barbecue tips!

MAKE A PLAN: Even if you're going low-key, spend just a bit of time planning and it will make all the difference to the end result. When you've decided what you want to eat, do as much prep beforehand as you can, then you can get the final bits on the barbecue when your guests arrive. If you're aiming for a bit of a feast, think about balancing all those delicious flavours and textures as you build your menu. So if your main dish packs a punch in terms of heat, introduce a cooling, creamy side. To balance sticky glazes, get some good crunch going on – that's why slaw is always such an incredible barbecue favourite. Having said all that, I do think that rules don't really apply to outside cooking, and anything goes …

GET ORGANISED: Gather everything you need together before you start cooking and set it on a clean surface near the barbecue. Remember you'll need plates and boards for putting prepped food on before you start, and for resting cooked food on once it's done. It's really important that you use separate plates and boards for uncooked and cooked meat or fish, so have several to hand.

BE CONFIDENT: Cooking over flame needs you to be bold, both with your flavours and attitude. You're not looking for subtlety here, just go for it. It is possible to over-spice food and make it too hot for some people, but I don't think you can ever have too much flavour. I have never heard anyone say, 'there's too much marinade', so don't hold back. And don't be intimidated by cooking over fire – it's very forgiving, you just need to keep an eye on it.

BE PATIENT: Barbecuing is about waiting, watching and reacting: waiting for the coals to reach the right temperature; watching as the food cooks and turning it over to cook on the other side at the right moment. Boosting the heat if the temperature drops, or moving the food to a cooler area if you think it's cooking too quickly; brushing on more glaze to layer up those flavours and taking the food off when you think it's ready. Barbecuing is a bit like taking the kids to the playground – you always need to have your eye on it, even if most of the time you're not actually doing much!

RELAX: Let's be honest, it's not a real barbecue until someone spills sauce down their front! Getting messy is part of it, so just stack up a load of napkins and get stuck in. Don't over-complicate things and don't stress. Let the cooking process take care of itself. There's no right or wrong way, just guidance – and with all those delicious marinades and spice rubs, as long as it's cooked everyone will enjoy it, so don't worry! Yes, we can all hope for a perfect sunny day but we can't rely on the weather, so don't let it deter you. There's nothing to stop you cooking in the colder months too – the pheasant, mushroom and pear kebabs on page 45 are made for autumn barbecuing.

How to cook over flames

One of the first things to understand when it comes to barbecuing is it needs patience. It's not like turning on the oven or grill, and 20 minutes later your dinner's ready. But that's all part of the fun of cooking outdoors. What better way to spend the afternoon than just hanging out by the barbecue in the sunshine, watching your food cook? You've no other place to be right now and no other responsibilities. It's almost quite zen-like.

WHAT KIND OF BARBECUE?

When it comes to deciding what kind of barbecue to use, it really depends how into it you're going to get!

Cooking over an open fire means you get amazing smoky flavours in your food. I love this way of cooking as it's so instinctive, but it's also much less predictable. You have to really pay attention, adding more wood to boost the fire and keep everything going at a steady heat. You wouldn't usually use it for barbecuing in a traditional style – you'll be more likely to put everything in a big pot or frying pan, or cook directly in the hot embers. You can read more about this in the Open Fire chapter on page 156.

Gas barbecues are reliable in terms of maintaining an even temperature, but you do miss out on all that great smoky flavour. You still get the lovely outdoors feeling, but I enjoy the back-to-basics feel of coal and wood.

Kettle (Weber-style) barbecues are very popular. These come with a lid that usually has air vents in it, which makes it easier to adjust the temperature. If you close the lid but leave the air vents open, it will help drive air up through the coals, helping them burn stronger and raising the temperature in the barbecue. If you leave the lid closed, but also close the air vents you'll achieve the opposite effect – the coals won't be getting extra oxygen, so they will start to cool off. Having a lid on your barbecue creates an oven-like environment, which is good for things like seafood or slow-cooked ribs – although you can get a similar effect by wrapping your ingredients with foil.

You can also get fancy temperature-controlled ceramic barbecues, such as The Big Green Egg or other kamado-style barbecues. Being made from ceramic helps keep the temperature inside consistent, which is especially good for slow-cooked recipes. These types of barbecues come with a temperature gauge, so you know roughly what heat you're at (the recipes in this book tend to be cooked at around 160°C or a bit hotter) but even so, there will always be cooler areas across the grill, so you still have to keep an eye on your food and move it around if you think it needs it.

Having an uneven heat can actually be very useful though – you can cook veg more slowly on the cooler areas, and sear meat or fish where it's hotter. I often move coals around to create a range of temperatures across the grill.

START COOKING

First, you want to let the coals heat up properly. You need a good airflow to get those coals burning and a reliable way to do that is to arrange them in a pyramid and light them from underneath. You can use scrunched-up newspaper or kindling to get the fire going, or odour-free firelighters. Once it's burning, leave until the flames die down and you have hot, glowing coals that are coated in ash. This should take around 25–30 minutes.

A bit of kit I think is worth investing in is a coal kettle, or chimney. It's a bit like a metal bucket with holes in the bottom that sits on top of your metal rack. You load it with coals then light some firelighters or kindling underneath. Oxygen gets drawn up through the chimney, which helps your coals burn evenly. In about 20 minutes, you'll have perfectly hot coals which you can carefully tip onto the barbecue. Spread them out, and you're ready to go!

If you're cooking several different things at the same time, you can arrange your coals in a way that gives a range of temperatures. A steak or lamb skewers will need to be cooked over a hotter, more direct heat than a whole aubergine or pieces of halloumi, for example. Use a pair of coal tongs to shift hot and cooler coals around when you need to adjust the heat; if the heat drops too low in one area, then scoot some of the hotter coals over. You can also increase the heat by closing the lid (if you have one) and letting air flow through the open vents.

I can't stress this enough: don't wander away! You need to stay close to your barbecue at all times. Partly so you don't accidentally cause a fire, but also to keep an eye on your food. The heat might drop out, or fat dripping onto the coals could make the flames really fire up, which will definitely burn your food!

Keep testing the heat of the barbecue by hovering your hand above it, and think about whether to increase or lower the heat, or move your food around. If you're cooking lots of different elements for a meal, you can keep things warm on cooler parts of the barbecue while you wait for the other bits to be ready – but really, I think it's best to serve them up as soon as they're cooked when they'll be at their best, and not worry about eating everything together. It's part of the fun of cooking outside!

Most of the time, you'll be cooking on the rack set above your hot coals. Barbecues usually have a couple of settings for this, so you can raise or lower the rack, depending on the level of heat you want. You can use saucepans and frying pans too – either on the rack or straight into the hot coals (or wood embers if you're on an open fire). It's a great way of introducing smoky flavour to more elements of your meal. I cook the sweet potato burgers on page 137 this way, and I even make a complete campfire breakfast in a pan set over the flames (see page 158). The pans will scorch over the flames, so don't use your best cooking pots, or anything flimsy over the intense heat.

Kit

It's easy to get carried away and spend a fortune on barbecue kit. If you're the kind of person who can't resist getting all the gear I'm not going to stop you! But you don't need loads of stuff to get started … just a few items.

CHARCOAL Unless you're cooking over an open wood fire, lumpwood charcoal or charcoal briquettes that come in a big bag will be the simplest and most easily available option. Some specify the kind of wood they use (like maple or hickory) so you can experiment with the extra flavour they add. You can also get bags of wood chips that you add to the barbecue for extra smoky flavour (see below).

COAL CHIMNEY You can get one of these for as little as a tenner, and it will save you time waiting for your coals to get to the right heat. It will also ensure an even heat across the coals.

FIRE LIGHTERS A quick way to get the flames started underneath the coals or coal chimney. Get some that are odour free so you don't end up with a chemical taste in the smoke.

COAL TONGS For moving the hot coals around to create a more even temperature or to make hot or cooler zones, depending on what you need. Make sure they're heat- and flameproof.

FIRE GLOVE It's essential to wear a heat-resistant glove when you're moving the grid or hot coals on the barbecue, or logs on an open fire.

COOKING TONGS You'll need long-handled tongs and a robust spatula for turning food over – make sure they're heat- and flameproof.

BRUSHES Have a few of these for oiling and glazing during cooking. If you are using different flavoured glazes, it's a good idea to keep a separate brush for each one.

FISH CAGE I love using a fish cage (also called a fish basket) to cook whole fish. It makes them easy to turn over and less likely to stick to the metal rack, and you can pack in a load of herbs and other aromatics for extra flavour.

MEAT THERMOMETER Using a digital probe themometer helps to avoid the risk of under- or over-cooking meat. It registers the internal temperature of the meat, which indicates when that's ready to take off the barbecue.

SPRAY BOTTLE OF WATER This will come in useful when you want to stop something caramelising too quickly, or if you want to create a bit of steam to help the cooking process.

WOOD CHIPS These can be a nice way of adding an extra flavour dimension to your barbecue. There are loads of options, so try out a few to see what you like. Fruitwoods are generally milder and better suited to more delicate fish and chicken. Oak and hickory give off a much headier smoky flavour, and so work well with more robust meat – like beef, pork and lamb.

To Start

SNACKS
TASTY
SHARING

TO START

When I'm putting on a barbecue, I like to get some food on the fire as soon as people arrive. Having a few sharing plates, a stack of skewers, or some bread and dips out there can tide everyone over and get people in the party mood. It also gives you time to put the finishing touches to the main event. This chapter is full of amazing starter-style dishes that can be cooked quickly on the grill – and you can eat a lot of them one-handed, leaving your other hand free to do the all-important work of holding on to your drink.

Most of these recipes have been inspired by the incredible diversity of street food you can experience around the world – snacky-type bites, often made to order and designed to eat on the move. Skewers are great for this, as they're so versatile – you can put almost anything on them. It's a chance to get the kids involved too. Get them to thread the ingredients on and turn the skewers on the barbecue, under your supervision. Remember if you're using wooden skewers to soak them in water first, to help stop them catching light as they cook.

You could make a whole menu out of these recipes, mix-and-matching them for a really relaxed meal rather than focussing on one big central dish. Don't worry about things not going with each other – it's all part of cooking and eating outside. Feel free to enjoy my Mexican quesadilla with some Mediterranean butterflied prawns, alongside a tasty pheasant, mushroom and pear kebab if that's what you want to do! (See pages 35, 36 and 45.) It's a chance to try something you might not have had before without having to commit to a whole main course.

Although I love how easy and relaxed barbecues can be, these starters and sharing plates will make it feel like you've really put in the effort and made it into a special occasion.

CHARRED PEACH, PARMA HAM *and* BOCCONCINI

serves 4

This play on the classic Parma ham and melon combination works so well because the sweetness of the peaches balances the saltiness from the ham and cheese. Peaches caramelise perfectly on the barbecue – go for fruit that are still a bit firm, so they don't collapse as they cook.

· ·

4 peaches (ripe but firm), halved and de-stoned

2 tbsp rapeseed oil

A large handful of rocket leaves

A large handful of watercress leaves

8 generous slices of Parma ham, cut in half

350g bocconcini (baby buffalo mozzarella)

DRESSING

½ red chilli, finely diced

1 red onion, finely diced

100ml extra virgin olive oil

40ml sherry vinegar

Salt and freshly ground black pepper

TO FINISH

4 tbsp flaked almonds, toasted

4 basil leaves, roughly chopped

1 Lay the peach halves, cut side up, on a tray and drizzle with the rapeseed oil.

2 When ready to cook, place each peach half, cut side down, on the hot barbecue and leave for 3 minutes until they have lovely charred marks on the underside. You just want to cook them briefly, to ensure they retain that kick of freshness. Carefully lift the peaches off the barbecue onto a tray and set aside until needed.

3 To make the dressing, mix the chilli, red onion, extra virgin olive oil and sherry vinegar together in a bowl. Season with a pinch each of salt and pepper.

4 Put 2 peach halves on each serving plate and surround with the rocket and watercress. Add the Parma ham and bocconcini. Spoon on the dressing and sprinkle over the toasted almonds and basil to serve.

TOFU *and* VEG SKEWERS

Tofu is an amazing ingredient because it acts like a flavour sponge. The soy, honey and sesame marinade for these skewers is absorbed by the tofu, and doubles as a deliciously sticky glaze. Courgettes and baby corn provide a lovely contrasting crunch.

400g firm tofu

150g baby corn

150g small courgettes

150g mushrooms

150g Romano peppers, halved, cored and deseeded

Salt

MARINADE

4 tbsp soy sauce (Kikkoman)

2 tbsp honey

5cm piece of fresh ginger, finely grated

2 tbsp sesame oil

1 tbsp rice wine vinegar

1 tbsp toasted sesame seeds

TO SERVE

2 spring onions, finely sliced

Sweet chilli dipping sauce

1 If using wooden skewers, pre-soak them in water for 30 minutes to avoid scorching on the barbecue.

2 Cut the tofu into 2cm cubes and place in a shallow dish. For the marinade, mix all the ingredients, except the sesame seeds, together in a bowl. Pour half of the marinade over the tofu, mix well and leave to marinate for 20 minutes, turning the cubes over at least once.

3 Add the toasted sesame seeds to the rest of the marinade and set aside for brushing on the skewers during cooking.

4 Bring a small saucepan of water to the boil over a high heat and season with a good pinch of salt. Add the corn and cook for 2–3 minutes. Drain and cool slightly.

5 Cut the baby corn, courgettes, mushrooms and peppers into 2cm pieces. Thread the marinated tofu and veg pieces onto 8 skewers, alternating them.

6 Place the skewers on a medium-hot barbecue and cook for around 10–12 minutes, brushing them regularly with the remaining marinade and turning them often. When the veg are lightly charred in places and cooked through, lift the skewers off the barbecue.

7 Place the skewers on a warmed serving platter. Scatter the sliced spring onions over them and serve at once, with sweet chilli dipping sauce.

TOMATO, BURRATA *and* ANCHOVY SALAD

A super-tasty salad of flavourful tomatoes, peppery watercress and rocket with two types of anchovies is topped with creamy burrata and drizzled with garlic and parsley dressing. Flatbreads, cooked on the grill, sit underneath and absorb all the delicious juices from the salad.

500g tomatoes (ideally mixed heritage)

½ red onion, thinly sliced

2 garlic cloves, thinly sliced

1 tsp flaky sea salt

3 tbsp olive oil

3 drops of Tabasco

Finely grated zest of ½ lemon

6 basil leaves, torn

A handful of watercress leaves

A large handful of rocket leaves

12 smoked anchovies

12 marinated anchovies in vinegar

2 x 200g burrata

GARLIC AND HERB FLATBREADS

250g strong white bread flour, plus extra to dust

¼ tsp salt

4 tbsp olive oil

110ml warm water

GARLIC AND PARSLEY OIL

80ml olive oil

2 garlic cloves, grated

1 tbsp chopped flat-leaf parsley

1 To prepare the flatbread dough, mix all the ingredients together in a bowl until smoothly combined and bring the dough together with your hands. Turn onto a lightly floured surface and knead well for a few minutes. Place in a bowl, cover and leave to rest for 30 minutes.

2 Meanwhile, halve or slice the tomatoes, depending on size, and place in a shallow bowl. Scatter over the red onion, garlic and salt. Leave to stand for 10–15 minutes.

3 For the garlic and parsley oil, heat the olive oil in a small pan over a low heat on the hob, then take off the heat and add the garlic. Let cool then stir in the parsley.

4 Divide the rested dough into 4 even-sized balls. Roll each one out thinly to make a large flatbread, sprinkle with flour and lay on top of each other, ready to barbecue.

5 When ready to serve, place the flatbreads on the hot barbecue for 1–2 minutes until puffed up and lightly charred on the underside. Flip the breads over and cook on the other side for a minute or two. Remove from the heat and brush with the garlic and parsley oil. Wrap in foil to keep warm.

6 By now, the tomatoes will have released some juice. Add the olive oil, Tabasco, lemon zest and basil to them, to create a flavourful dressing.

7 To serve, lay a flatbread on each plate and cover with the salad leaves, tomato salad and anchovies. Cut the burrata in half and place cut side up on the salad. Spoon over any remaining dressing and serve.

SMOKED AUBERGINE DIP *and* SPICED FLATBREADS

In this version of a popular dish we make at The Hand & Flowers, cooking aubergine on the barbecue enhances all its natural smoky flavours. Using toasted spices in the dip and cumin seeds in the flatbreads will bring a real taste of the Middle East to your plate.

3 large aubergines

2 tbsp cumin seeds, toasted

2 tbsp coriander seeds, toasted

2–3 tbsp olive oil

200ml double cream

Finely grated zest and juice of 1 large lemon

Salt and cayenne pepper

SPICED FLATBREADS

280g self-raising flour, plus extra to dust

250g natural yoghurt

2 tbsp extra virgin olive oil

1 tsp cumin seeds

½ tsp salt

4 tbsp garlic-infused oil

TO SERVE (OPTIONAL)

Baby cucumbers, blanched asparagus spears, radishes and carrots, halved lengthways

1 Lay the aubergines on the hot barbecue and cook until the skin is blistered and charred all over, turning every few minutes. Transfer to a tray and let cool slightly, then split open with a knife and scrape the flesh from the skins. Spoon into a colander and leave to drain for 30 minutes or so, then tip the aubergine flesh onto a clean board and chop finely. Place in a sieve to drain off the juice.

2 Using a pestle and mortar, grind the toasted spice seeds to a fine powder. Place a cast-iron pan on the barbecue to warm up, then add the olive oil. Tip in the ground spices and stir until they release their aroma. Stir in the chopped aubergine. Cook for 5–8 minutes, stirring to drive off as much liquid as possible. Take off the heat and stir in the cream and lemon zest and juice. Season with salt and cayenne to taste and spoon into a serving bowl; set aside.

3 To prepare the flatbread dough, mix all the ingredients, except the garlic-infused oil, together in a bowl until smoothly combined and bring the dough together with your hands. Turn onto a lightly floured surface and knead well for a few minutes. Place in a bowl, cover and leave to rest for 30 minutes. Once rested, divide the dough into 6 even-sized balls. Roll each one out thinly, sprinkle with flour and lay on top of each other, ready to barbecue.

4 Just before serving, cook the flatbreads on the barbecue for 1–2 minutes on each side until puffed and blistered. Lift off and brush with the garlic-infused oil. Cut into pieces.

5 Serve the smoked aubergine dip with the hot flatbreads and veggies for dipping.

BEETROOT CARPACCIO

Creamy, salty feta and earthy, roasted beetroot: it's a pairing we all know works. The dressing provides a lovely chilli kick and acidity (from the sherry vinegar) to balance those flavours out. Serve the beetroot carpaccio on its own or with white fish or chicken.

1.6kg medium beetroot (ideally, use an assortment of varieties, such as red, golden and candy-striped chiogga)

3 tbsp extra virgin olive oil

½ long red chilli, deseeded and finely diced

½ tsp onion seeds

1½ tbsp sherry vinegar

100g sheep's feta or soft goat's cheese

A handful of mint leaves

20g roasted hazelnuts

1 tbsp pomegranate molasses

Salt and freshly ground black pepper

1 You can roast beetroot directly on white-hot coals if you want to get as much smoky flavour inside them as possible. Or, alternatively, you can wrap them in foil and place them on the barbecue or onto the coals. Cook for around 40–50 minutes, depending on their size, until tender, turning them regularly, every 5–10 minutes or so. To check they are cooked, pierce with a skewer – it should pass though easily.

2 Leave the beetroot to cool slightly and then rub off the skins with your fingers. You can do this under running cold water if you like to ensure all the burnt bits come off easily. Slice the beetroot thinly and arrange in a shallow serving bowl.

3 Heat the olive oil in a small cast-iron pan over the barbecue then remove the pan from the heat and immediately add the red chilli and onion seeds. Leave to sizzle gently for a minute, then add the sherry vinegar and some seasoning and leave this dressing to cool slightly.

4 Break up the feta or goat's cheese into bite-sized pieces and distribute evenly over the beetroot. Spoon the dressing over the barbecued beetroot and scatter over the mint leaves and roasted hazelnuts. Drizzle with the pomegranate molasses to serve.

TIP

Try to get even-sized beetroot so they will take around the same time to cook through.

THREE CHEESE QUESADILLAS

Each cheese brings its own unique qualities to these deliciously rich quesadillas: mozzarella goes gooey and stretchy, Cheddar lends a sharp saltiness, while blue cheese offers punchy acidity. You'll find the tortilla crisps up as it cooks, which delivers a great mix of textures.

1 tbsp olive oil

30g butter

4 garlic cloves, sliced

300g chestnut mushrooms, thickly sliced

4 large flour tortillas

80g blue cheese, finely crumbled

120g mozzarella, grated

120g Cheddar, grated

3 fresh jalapeño chillies, thickly sliced

Olive oil to brush

Salt and freshly ground black pepper

Mixed salad leaves to serve

1 Heat the olive oil and butter in a cast-iron pan on your hot barbecue. When hot, add the garlic to the pan and stir for a minute or so, until sizzling gently. Now add the mushrooms and season with salt and pepper. Cook for 4–5 minutes or until they are softened and browned. Take the pan off the heat and leave to cool a little.

2 Lay each tortilla out flat and make a cut from the centre to the bottom outer edge. In your mind, divide the tortilla into quarters. Distribute the blue cheese over the upper left-hand quarter and scatter the mushrooms on top. Fold the bottom left-hand corner of the tortilla up over the blue cheese and mushroom layer to enclose it.

3 Scatter the mozzarella over the top right quarter then fold the top left (filled) quarter over to enclose. Lastly, sprinkle the Cheddar and sliced jalapeños over the top right (filled) quarter and fold the bottom right quarter up and over to enclose all the filling.

4 Brush the folded tortillas lightly with olive oil and place on the barbecue where you can achieve a medium heat. You don't want them to brown too quickly before the cheese has melted, so keep a close eye on them.

5 Once the cheese has melted and the tortillas are golden brown, lift them off the barbecue and serve with a mixed salad alongside.

BUTTERFLIED GARLIC *and* CHILLI PRAWNS

This is like barbecuing mini lobsters! Use large prawns with shells still on – the roasted flavour of the shells will make its way into the prawns as they cook. If you brush on plenty of garlic and chilli butter, it'll keep them deliciously juicy. A squeeze of lime cuts the richness beautifully.

• •

16 extra-large raw prawns (about 800g in total)

GARLIC AND CHILLI BUTTER

150g butter

2 garlic cloves, finely chopped

1 red chilli, deseeded and finely diced

Finely grated zest of ½ lime

2 tbsp finely chopped coriander leaves

Salt and freshly ground black pepper

TO FINISH AND SERVE

Coriander leaves, roughly chopped

Lime wedges

Crusty bread

1 First, prepare the prawns. Uncurl a prawn so it's facing belly side up. Using a sharp knife, make a cut from the head to the tip of the tail, through the meat but not the outer shell. Open the prawn up and flatten it out. This will expose the black intestinal tract – prise this out with the tip of your knife and discard it. Repeat with the rest of the prawns. Place the prawns, cut side down, on a tray and pop them in the fridge while you make the garlic and chilli butter.

2 Put the butter into a small pan over a medium heat on the hob. When melted and sizzling, add the garlic and cook for 1 minute. Add the chilli and cook for another minute. Remove from the heat and stir in the lime zest and chopped coriander. Season well with salt and pepper.

3 Turn the prawns over, so they are cut side up and brush the meat with the butter. Put them back into the fridge until you are ready to barbecue.

4 When you are ready to cook the prawns, place them shell side down on a medium-hot barbecue and cook for 2 minutes. Then flip them over and cook flesh side down for 2–3 minutes. The butter will drop into the coals a little at this point and cause a bit of smoke to rise up but don't worry – this is all part of the fun of barbecuing.

5 Once the prawns are cooked, place them on a warmed platter and give the flesh side an extra brush of butter. Sprinkle with a little chopped coriander and serve at once, with lime wedges. Eat the prawns straight away, grabbing some crusty bread to mop up all that delicious butter.

SCALLOPS WITH LIME *and* LEMONGRASS BUTTER

makes 12

To fully appreciate the delicate, sweet taste of scallops you need to treat them simply. They're just cooked in their shells in this recipe, in butter flavoured with lemongrass, lime leaves and coriander – a nod to fresh Thai-style flavours.

12 scallops, cleaned and in their half-shells

LIME AND LEMONGRASS BUTTER

200g butter, softened

6 kaffir lime leaves, finely chopped

3 tsp lemongrass paste

2 tsp fish sauce

2 tbsp finely chopped coriander leaves

Salt and freshly ground white pepper

TO FINISH AND SERVE

A few spring onions, green part only, finely shredded

Lime wedges

1 Make sure both the scallops and their shells are clean. For the flavoured butter, in a small bowl, mix the butter with the chopped lime leaves, lemongrass paste, fish sauce and chopped coriander. Season with a good pinch each of salt and white pepper. Mix well.

2 Lift a scallop up a little in its shell and put a teaspoonful of the butter underneath it then carefully spread another teaspoonful on top. Repeat with the rest of the scallops.

3 Place the scallops in their shells on the hot barbecue grid; the butter will sizzle and cook them. They will only take around 3 minutes to cook through; turn each scallop over in its shell halfway through cooking.

4 If you'd like a little caramelisation on the scallops, lift them out of their shells towards the end of cooking and place them directly on the barbecue. Cook for 20 seconds or so on each side then return the scallops to the shells.

5 Once cooked, lift the scallop shells onto a tray. Sprinkle shredded spring onion over the scallops and serve with lime wedges for squeezing. Tuck in straight away!

SQUID *and* CHORIZO SKEWERS

makes **8**

For a taste of Spanish holidays, charred squid is paired with Padrón peppers and spicy chorizo, then served with a cooling lemony mayo. Don't be afraid of barbecuing squid – it's easy and cooks quickly, so these skewers are ideal for getting on the grill when your guests arrive.

· ·

500g medium squid with tentacles, cleaned

Finely grated zest of 1 lemon

2 tbsp extra virgin olive oil

2 large garlic cloves, finely grated

2 tbsp finely chopped flat-leaf parsley

2 rosemary sprigs, finely chopped

200g spicy cooking chorizo sausage, cut into 2cm chunks

200g Padrón peppers

Salt and freshly ground black pepper

LEMON MAYO

100g mayonnaise

50g Greek yoghurt

Juice of ½ lemon

1 small garlic clove, finely grated

TO SERVE

4 large flatbreads, cut into quarters

120g rocket leaves

1 lemon, cut into wedges

1 If using wooden skewers, pre-soak them in water for 30 minutes to avoid scorching on the barbecue.

2 On a board, carefully slice open each squid pouch so it lies flat and cut a lattice pattern on the softer, internal surface. Cut the squid pouches into 5cm pieces. Cut the tentacles in half.

3 Put the scored squid and tentacles into a small bowl and add the lemon zest, extra virgin olive oil, garlic, herbs and some seasoning. Leave to marinate for 15 minutes.

4 Meanwhile, in a bowl, mix all the ingredients together for the lemon mayo and set aside.

5 Thread the marinated squid, chorizo chunks and Padrón peppers alternately onto 8 skewers. Place on a hot barbecue and cook for 6–8 minutes, turning frequently. Towards the end of cooking, briefly place the flatbreads on the barbecue to warm through, turning them once.

6 Serve the skewers as soon as they are ready, with the lemon mayo, rocket and lemon wedges alongside.

BARBECUED PRAWN *and* AVOCADO COCKTAILS

serves 4

Chargrilling tiger prawns takes the seventies classic prawn cocktail to a whole new level! Celery adds a delicious crispness to the salad and smooth, creamy avocado counters the spicy heat and acidity in the Marie Rose sauce.

600g large raw tiger prawns

3 tbsp extra virgin olive oil

1 large garlic clove, finely chopped

2 tbsp finely chopped flat-leaf parsley

6 dashes of Tabasco

Juice of ½ lemon

Salt and freshly ground black pepper

MARIE ROSE SAUCE

120ml mayonnaise

60ml tomato ketchup

1 tbsp brandy

5 dashes of Worcestershire sauce

6 dashes of Tabasco

Juice of ½ lemon

SALAD

1 small iceberg lettuce

2 celery sticks, finely sliced

1 ripe avocado

TO FINISH

2 tbsp finely chopped chives

1 lemon, cut into wedges

1 First, peel the prawns, removing the heads but leaving the tail shells on. Using a sharp knife, make a small slit along the middle of the back to expose the dark intestinal vein. Prise this out with the tip of your knife and discard it.

2 Put the prawns into a bowl and add the extra virgin olive oil, garlic, parsley, Tabasco, lemon juice and some seasoning. Mix well and leave to marinate for 10 minutes.

3 Meanwhile, make the Marie Rose sauce: mix all the ingredients together in a small bowl and season with salt and pepper to taste. Cover and place in the fridge until needed.

4 Cut the lettuce into quarters and use the outer leaves to line 4 serving bowls. Thinly slice the rest of the lettuce and put it into a large bowl with the celery.

5 To cook the prawns, lay them on a hot barbecue and cook for 2–3 minutes on each side, depending on size (and the heat). Transfer to a tray and leave to cool slightly.

6 Add a couple of spoonfuls of Marie Rose sauce to the shredded lettuce and celery, season with salt and pepper to taste and toss to mix.

7 Halve, peel, de-stone and cut the avocado into quarters. Divide the sliced lettuce and celery between serving bowls and spoon on a generous amount of Marie Rose sauce. Pile the barbecued prawns on top and tuck an avocado wedge into each bowl. Finish with the chopped chives and serve with lemon wedges.

PHEASANT, MUSHROOM *and* PEAR KEBABS

makes 4

Barbecueing outdoors is not just for summer. These quick-cook kebabs are ideal for the colder months when pheasant is in season. The colourful chicory, pear, walnut and blue cheese side salad is like an autumn version of slaw.

. . . .

4 boneless pheasant breasts, skinned

2 large pears (ripe but firm), halved and cored (skin on)

2 portobello mushrooms, cut into chunks

A bunch of rosemary

MARINADE

50ml cold-pressed rapeseed oil

75ml Perry (or pear cider)

5 juniper berries, crushed

½ tsp thyme leaves

½ tsp salt

2 tsp chopped Douglas fir pine or rosemary

HONEY GLAZE

75ml honey

150ml Perry (or pear cider)

100ml chicken stock

50g butter

SALAD

2 red chicory bulbs, leaves separated

2 white chicory bulbs, leaves separated

1 pear, halved, cored and sliced

3 tbsp olive oil

50g crumbly blue cheese

50g toasted chopped walnuts or pecan nuts, lightly crushed

1 Cut the pheasant breasts into bite-sized (2cm) pieces. Combine the ingredients for the marinade in a bowl, add the pheasant pieces and toss to coat, then cover and place in the fridge for 1 hour.

2 Drain the pheasant, saving the marinade. Cut the pears into 2cm pieces. Thread the pheasant onto 4–6 metal skewers, alternating with the pear and mushroom pieces. Place the kebabs on a tray, pour on the marinade and add the rosemary sprigs. Cover and refrigerate until needed.

3 For the glaze, heat the honey in a small cast-iron pan on the barbecue until it starts to caramelise, then carefully pour in the Perry and stock. Let bubble rapidly for around 10 minutes until reduced and thickened to a light syrup. Stir in the butter and take the pan off the heat.

4 Lay the kebabs on the barbecue on a medium-high heat and cook for 4 minutes, brushing with a little of the marinade if you think they need a little oil during cooking. Turn the kebabs over and brush with the honey glaze. Cook for a further 4 minutes; the glaze will char slightly and caramelise, lending a bitter-sweet flavour.

5 Once cooked, transfer the kebabs to a warmed plate or board, cover with foil and leave to rest for 5 minutes.

6 Meanwhile, for the salad, arrange the chicory and pear on a platter and drizzle with the olive oil. Crumble the blue cheese on top and scatter over the toasted nuts. Trickle the remaining glaze over the warm kebabs and serve straight away, with the salad.

GLAZED PORK SKEWERS *with* PICKLED MOOLI

makes 12

Full of Japanese flavours, these pork belly skewers are sticky, sweet and unbelievably delicious. Mooli is like a giant, mild radish. Lightly pickled with kombu, it is the perfect complement to the skewers – providing a fresh, slightly peppery crunch.

500g pork belly, skin removed

8 spring onions, cut into 4cm lengths

PICKLED MOOLI

300g mooli, peeled and finely sliced

5cm piece of kombu

150ml rice wine vinegar

2 tsp salt

100g caster sugar

SOY, HONEY AND GINGER GLAZE

4 tbsp soy sauce (Kikkoman)

2 tbsp mirin

2 tbsp honey

2.5cm piece of fresh ginger, peeled and finely chopped

Salt and freshly ground white pepper

TO FINISH (OPTIONAL)

Togarashi seasoning to sprinkle

1 Prepare the pickled mooli at least an hour ahead. Put the sliced mooli into a clean 500ml jar. Combine the kombu, rice wine vinegar, salt and sugar in a saucepan and bring to a simmer over a low heat. Stir until the sugar and salt are both dissolved and then pour the liquid over the mooli. Leave to cool. Put the lid on and refrigerate until needed.

2 Pre-soak 12 short wooden skewers (about 12cm long) in water for 30 minutes to avoid scorching on the barbecue. Cut the pork belly into 4cm wide strips and cut each strip into 1cm slices. Thread these onto the skewers, alternating with the pieces of spring onion, so that each skewer has 3 pieces of pork and 3 pieces of spring onion.

3 For the glaze, put the soy sauce, mirin and honey into a small saucepan. Add the ginger along with a big pinch each of salt and white pepper. Bring to the boil over a high heat and cook for 2–3 minutes or until the sauce is slightly thickened. Remove from the heat and leave to cool.

4 Place the skewers on the barbecue over a medium heat and cook for 1 minute on each side before starting to brush each side with the glaze (this will prevent the glaze from burning before the pork has cooked through). Cook for a further 6–7 minutes, turning the skewers and glazing them as you go. (Keep them away from intense heat.) You will get a few little charred bits on the pork which is what you want as it enhances the flavour.

5 For a fiery kick, if you like, sprinkle the pork skewers with a little togarashi seasoning before serving, with the pickled mooli alongside.

JUICY

GLAZED

SMOKY

MEAT

There's a reason that cooking meat on the barbecue is so universally popular – it tastes amazing! There's nothing quite like that irresistible smoky flavour and delicious dark crust. It's all down to the intense heat from the coals caramelising the sugars and amino acids on the surface of the meat. If I could cook every steak on a barbecue, I would. You just can't beat the taste.

Cooking for other people is usually a case of aiming to keep everyone happy, so I always go for the crowd pleasers. You're never going to disappoint if you have a burger, some chicken, ribs or a steak on the menu. But that doesn't mean it has to be predictable. Meat is very forgiving and can stand up to some really bold flavours, so it gives you the perfect opportunity to play around with marinades, rubs and glazes. Try a spicy pork burger with Romanesco salsa for a Mediterranean twist on

a barbecue favourite, or my smoky pastrami burgers, which are inspired by those fantastic New York delis (see pages 95 and 75).

People often ask what my favourite thing to cook on a barbecue is – how much time do you have?! There are too many. But I do think chicken is probably the most versatile meat and the ingredient I'd come back to – it's the most accessible one too.

Meat with a higher fat content will always cook well on the barbecue because it will stay nice and juicy, so that's why I like to use chicken thighs – try them in the Thai-style skewers on page 58. If you're cooking a steak then go for a thick one with a good marbling of fat. By the time you get all that lovely caramelisation on the outside, if your steak is too thin the middle will be overdone – and you definitely don't want that! It doesn't mean you can't barbecue thinner cuts

(I use bavette steaks in the Korean Barbecued Beef on page 76); you'll just need to keep a bit more of a careful eye on them to make sure the meat doesn't dry out, and brush it with extra marinade or a glaze while it cooks to keep it tender. If you have a lidded temperature-controlled barbecue, then the whole chicken cooked over a beer can (page 62) makes a great summer alternative to a Sunday roast. The beer boils and steams the chicken inside, keeping it juicy. It looks really impressive too!

It's hard to top the barbecue classic meat-and-bread combo, and as well as burgers there are plenty of versions everywhere for you to try in this chapter – from a barbecued chicken BLT to the ultimate hot dog and a Vietnamese bánh mì (see pages 52, 82 and 88). The range of flavours from around the world in just these recipes shows how much people enjoy this kind of eating!

When it comes to cooking meat on the barbecue, it's hard to get it wrong so just enjoy it. All the flavours you add will only enhance the natural smokiness of the cooked meat. The only mistake people tend to make is thinking that they can just chuck all the food on and wander away – you do have to stay and watch it cook, otherwise you run the risk of it burning on the outside and being uncooked in the middle. That classic barbecue fail! This is where a meat thermometer comes in handy.

Barbecuing is all about touch and feel, and knowing when things are cooked is something you will learn quickly, but it's good to have a digital probe thermometer that allows you to check the internal temperature of a thick piece of meat. And remember, that temperature will continue to rise after you've taken the meat off the barbecue and set it aside to rest.

BARBECUED CHICKEN BLT

serves **4**

One of the nation's best-loved sandwiches has been given an upgrade by adding chicken that's been cooked on the barbecue to take on that irresistible flame-grilled taste. Full of fresh, light flavours, the herby mustard mayo is amazing with the smoky bacon.

8 skinless, boneless chicken thighs

2 garlic cloves, thinly sliced

2 rosemary sprigs, leaves picked and finely chopped

2 tbsp olive oil

8 rashers of smoked streaky bacon

Salt and freshly ground black pepper

HERBY MUSTARD MAYO

4 tbsp mayonnaise

2 tbsp soured cream

2 tbsp finely chopped dill leaves

3 dashes of Worcestershire sauce

2 dashes of hot sauce

2 tsp mild American mustard

A pinch of cayenne pepper

TO ASSEMBLE

4 large seeded brioche burger buns

2 ripe avocados

2 large tomatoes, sliced

2 little gem lettuce, leaves separated

1 Flatten the chicken thighs between two sheets of baking paper by bashing with a rolling pin until they are about 1cm thick; remove the paper.

2 Lay the chicken thighs in a shallow dish and add the garlic, rosemary and olive oil. Season with salt and pepper and rub the herby garlicky oil into the chicken. Set aside to marinate.

3 For the herby mustard mayo, mix all the ingredients together in a bowl and season with salt and a little pepper; set aside.

4 Your barbecue will be ready to cook the chicken once the embers have cooled down a bit. First, cut the burger buns in half and toast on your barbecue until lightly charred. Remove and set aside.

5 Lay the chicken thighs on the barbecue and cook for 3–4 minutes on each side (depending on the heat of your barbecue) until tender, adding the bacon as you turn the chicken. The rashers will take around 1 minute on each side. Once cooked, remove the chicken and bacon from the barbecue and place on a tray to rest. Halve, peel, de-stone and slice the avocados.

6 To assemble the burgers, spread some herby mayo on the bottom of each burger bun and add a couple of chicken thighs. Layer the tomato, bacon, avocado and lettuce on top. Spread another spoonful of mayo on the top half of each bun. Sandwich together and serve.

SHAWARMA CHICKEN WRAP

Not just a late-night snack on the way home from the pub, here kebabs are given the respect they deserve. They come with charred chilli sauce, cooling tahini yoghurt and a bit of crunchy cabbage. It's worth making the flatbreads too, as they really round the whole thing off.

• •

800g skinless, boneless chicken thighs
300g red cabbage
Juice of ½ lemon
Salt and freshly ground black pepper

MARINADE

1 heaped tsp ground cumin
1 tsp ground coriander
1 tsp hot smoked paprika
1 heaped tsp sumac
½ tsp ground cinnamon
2 heaped tsp Baharat spice blend
3 tbsp yoghurt

CHARRED CHILLI SAUCE

1 whole garlic bulb
2 tbsp extra virgin olive oil
1 red onion, halved (skin on)
2 red peppers
2 tomatoes
2 long red chillies
2 long green chillies
1 tbsp sherry vinegar

TAHINI YOGHURT

200g natural yoghurt
1–2 tbsp tahini
Juice of ½ lemon

TO SERVE

Yoghurt flatbreads (page 144)
Pickled chillies

1 Cut the chicken thighs into 4cm pieces. Mix the marinade ingredients together in a bowl. Add the chicken and season liberally with salt and pepper. Mix well and leave to marinate for 1–2 hours. Finely shred the red cabbage, toss with the lemon juice and set aside to pickle.

2 For the sauce, put the garlic bulb on a piece of foil, drizzle with a little of the olive oil and wrap to seal. Place on the hot barbecue with the onion and peppers. Cook, turning the veg carefully for 10 minutes, then add the tomatoes and chillies and cook all the veg until charred all over. As each item is cooked, transfer to a bowl; keep tightly covered with cling film.

3 Let the charred veg steam in the bowl for 5–10 minutes, then remove and peel away their skins. Halve and deseed the peppers and chillies then chop all the veg finely and place in a bowl. Squeeze out the flesh from 4 roasted garlic cloves, finely chop and add to the veg. Mix in the sherry vinegar, olive oil and a little seasoning.

4 For the tahini yoghurt, squeeze the flesh from 2 roasted garlic cloves and chop finely. Mix with the yoghurt, tahini, lemon juice and salt and pepper to taste.

5 Thread the chicken onto 6 metal skewers. Barbecue for 4–5 minutes on each side. Also, heat the flatbreads on the barbecue, for 1–2 minutes on each side.

6 Serve the chicken skewers with the warm flatbreads, chilli sauce, pickled cabbage, tahini yoghurt and pickled chillies.

BARBECUED CHICKEN WINGS THREE WAYS

serves **4 – 6**

Chicken wings are a barbecue classic but often they're smothered in an overly sweet sauce. These three glazes are light, fresh and packed with punchy flavours. Choose one or make all three then pile them high for everyone to dig in. Get those napkins ready!

• •

20 large chicken wings, jointed

200g table salt

2 litres water

10 black peppercorns

4 bay leaves

KOREAN-STYLE GLAZE

80ml rice vinegar

60g caster sugar

50ml Sriracha hot sauce

50ml tomato ketchup

2 tbsp gochujang chilli paste

2 tbsp sesame oil

20g butter

HONEY SOY GLAZE

100g runny honey

2 tbsp soy sauce (Kikkoman)

2 garlic cloves, finely grated

1 tbsp sesame oil

MUSTARD AND MAPLE GLAZE

75g butter, softened

1 tbsp cider vinegar

2 tbsp wholegrain mustard

80ml maple syrup

TO FINISH

2–3 spring onions (green part only)

Black sesame seeds

Toasted (white) sesame seeds

1 First brine the chicken. In a large bowl, whisk the salt into the water to dissolve and add the peppercorns and bay leaves. Immerse the chicken wings in the brine and place in the fridge overnight. Remove the wings from the brine and pat dry with kitchen paper.

2 To make the Korean-style glaze, put all the ingredients into a pan on the hob, bring to a simmer and cook for about 5 minutes, then take off the heat. For the honey soy glaze, whisk all the ingredients together in a bowl and set aside. For the mustard and maple glaze, melt the butter together with the cider vinegar, mustard and maple syrup in a pan over a low heat. Stir to combine; keep warm.

3 Place the chicken wings on a hot barbecue and cook for 10–12 minutes until slightly browned on each side, turning at least once. Now glaze each third of the wings with one of the glazes. Cook for a further minute or so, then turn and glaze the other side. Cook, turn and glaze the wings for another 3–4 minutes until slightly charred.

4 Remove the chicken wings from the barbecue and place them on a warmed tray. Brush generously with extra glaze and leave to rest for a minute or so. Meanwhile, finely shred the spring onions.

5 Garnish the Korean-style chicken wings with the black sesame seeds and shredded spring onion. Sprinkle the honey soy glazed wings with toasted sesame seeds. (Leave the maple and mustard glazed chicken wings plain.) Let everyone help themselves.

THAI CHICKEN SKEWERS *and* GREEN PAPAYA SALAD

serves 2

Inspired by Thai street food, these chicken skewers are infused with the flavours of tamarind, lemongrass and kaffir lime leaves. But it's the green papaya that's the star of the show, providing texture and acidity to balance the sticky marinade.

• •

500g skinless, boneless chicken thighs

1 tbsp tamarind paste

1 tsp lemongrass paste

2 tbsp Thai soy sauce

1 tbsp fish sauce

Juice of ½ lime

2 tbsp palm sugar, crumbled

3cm piece of fresh ginger, finely grated

3 kaffir lime leaves, finely chopped

GREEN PAPAYA SALAD

250g green papaya

1 small shallot, thinly sliced

1 long red chilli, finely chopped

1 bird's eye red chilli, thinly sliced

1 garlic clove, finely chopped

1 tbsp palm sugar

3 tbsp lime juice

2 tbsp fish sauce

8 cherry tomatoes, halved

80g green beans, trimmed and halved

A handful of coriander leaves

A handful of mint leaves

TO FINISH

30g salted roasted peanuts, roughly chopped

Lime wedges

1 Cut each chicken thigh into 4 equal pieces. Place in a bowl with the tamarind paste, lemongrass paste, soy sauce, fish sauce, lime juice, palm sugar, ginger and chopped lime leaves. Mix well and leave to marinate for at least 20 minutes.

2 Meanwhile, for the salad, peel and halve the papaya, then scrape out the seeds and cut the flesh into julienne strips. Place in a bowl and set aside.

3 Using a pestle and mortar, pound the shallot, chillies, garlic, palm sugar, lime juice and fish sauce together well to create the dressing.

4 Add your dressing to the bowl of green papaya, along with the tomatoes and green beans. Mix well, so the ingredients soak up all the amazing flavours of the dressing.

5 Thread the chicken pieces onto 4 metal skewers. Cook them on the hot barbecue for about 4–5 minutes on each side or until charred and cooked through.

6 Just before serving, roughly chop the coriander and mint and add to the salad. Toss to mix.

7 Divide the green papaya salad between serving plates and place the chicken skewers alongside. Sprinkle with peanuts for extra crunch and serve with lime wedges.

HERBY LEMON CHICKEN THIGHS

This simple chicken dish is a real taste of the Mediterranean, with fresh herbs, extra virgin olive oil and a citrusy tang from preserved lemons. To add to the sunny flavours, I like to serve a colourful Greek salad (see page 212) on the side.

· ·

12 boneless chicken thighs (skin on)

50ml extra virgin olive oil

50g preserved lemon, finely chopped

4 garlic cloves, finely grated

3 tbsp oregano leaves, roughly chopped

2 tbsp rosemary leaves, roughly chopped

Salt and freshly ground black pepper

Lemon wedges, to serve

1 Lay the chicken thighs in a shallow dish. Pour over the olive oil and add the preserved lemon, garlic and herbs. Sprinkle generously with salt and grind over some pepper. Mix well with your hands to ensure the chicken is evenly coated with the marinade. Cover the dish with cling film and place in the fridge to marinate for at least 30 minutes.

2 Take the chicken out of the fridge about 15 minutes before you will be ready to cook.

3 Lay the chicken thighs skin side down on a hot barbecue – try to position them close to but not directly over the coals, as the fat may drip down and cause the coals to flame up.

4 Move the chicken thighs around and turn them as they cook. They will take around 15–20 minutes to cook through, depending on how hot your barbecue is. To test, pierce the thickest part of the thigh with a skewer; if the juices run clear, the chicken is cooked.

5 Serve the chicken thighs with lemon wedges. A Greek salad goes brilliantly as a side dish.

BEER-CAN CHICKEN *with* GOCHUJANG BUTTER

serves **4**

For this barbecue twist on a traditional Sunday roast chicken – brushed with garlicky chilli butter and served with kimchi – you really need to use a lidded temperature-controlled barbecue. Brining the chicken first and then cooking it with the beer helps keep it tender.

A 2kg whole chicken, giblets removed

440ml can beer

Flaky sea salt and freshly ground white pepper

GOCHUJANG BUTTER

80g butter, softened

2 tbsp gochujang paste

2 garlic cloves, finely grated

1 tbsp soy sauce (Kikkoman)

1 tbsp fish sauce

1 tsp sesame oil

1 tsp caster sugar

TO SERVE

1–2 red chillies, finely sliced

6 tbsp Japanese mayo (or use 6 tbsp classic mayonnaise mixed with 1 tbsp rice wine vinegar and ½ tsp sugar)

Kimchi

1 Season the chicken all over with salt and pepper. Open the can of beer and pour out half of the beer – feel free to drink it! Leave the rest in the can – it will help to keep the chicken moist as it cooks. Sit the chicken upright on the can, so it is partly inside the cavity. If the legs hang down too far, tie them up with kitchen string to stop them burning.

2 Fit the convector plate in your temperature-controlled barbecue and heat to 190°C. Lift the chicken (and can) onto the convector plate so it starts to cook.

3 Meanwhile place all the ingredients for the gochujang butter in a small cast-iron pan on the barbecue and stir until the butter is melted and the sugar dissolved. Remove from the heat and set aside.

4 After 10 minutes' cooking, brush the chicken with the marinade and put the lid on the barbecue, so that it functions more like an oven. It should take around 1 hour to cook, depending on the heat of your barbecue. Baste the chicken with the butter every 10 minutes or so, putting the lid back on each time. The chicken should be well browned and the skin should be charred in places. To check that it's cooked through, pierce the thickest part of the thigh with a skewer – the juices should run clear.

5 Remove the chicken from the barbecue and place it in a roasting tin, discarding the beer can. Cover the bird with foil and leave it to rest for 20 minutes.

6 Carve the chicken and garnish with sliced red chillies. Serve with some Japanese mayo and kimchi alongside.

CÔTE DE BOEUF *with* BLUE CHEESE SAUCE

CÔTE DE BOEUF *with* BLUE CHEESE SAUCE

serves 2

Steak and blue cheese sauce is always a winning combo. Blue cheese has a punchy tangy acidity, which balances the richness of the buttery, garlicky steak. Cooking your potatoes directly in the coals gives them an intensely smoky taste.

• •

1 côte de boeuf (bone in), about 600g, at room temperature

20ml vegetable oil

150g butter

2 garlic cloves, lightly smashed

2 rosemary sprigs

2 thyme sprigs

Juice of 1 lemon

Salt

BLUE CHEESE SAUCE

125g Gorgonzola (or any soft blue cheese)

100ml crème fraîche

50g mayonnaise

Cayenne pepper, to taste

1 tbsp chopped chives

BAKED POTATOES

300g large new potatoes (about 8)

2 tbsp vegetable oil

2 tsp salt

TO GARNISH

12 asparagus spears

1 Prepare the blue cheese sauce ahead. Crumble the cheese into a bowl, add the crème fraîche and mayonnaise and beat together until smoothly blended. Season with cayenne and a little salt if needed and stir in the chives. Cover and keep in the fridge. Before serving, spoon the sauce into a serving bowl and bring back to room temperature.

2 Create a bit of space for your potatoes among the hot coals towards the front of your barbecue. On a tray, toss the potatoes in the oil and salt to coat, then carefully place them directly on the coals, protecting your hands as you do so. Or, if you prefer, first wrap the potatoes individually in foil. Cook for about 15 minutes, turning regularly. To test, pierce the potatoes with a skewer to make sure they are soft.

3 Drizzle the steak with the oil and season heavily with salt. Lay the steak on a medium-hot part of your barbecue and cook for about 10 minutes, then turn over and repeat on the other side. Once both sides are coloured, hold the steak upright with tongs so that the edges colour too.

4 When the potatoes have had 15 minutes' cooking, remove them from the barbecue. If you've placed them directly in the coals they will have a little soot on them, but that's ok. Leave them to stand for about 10 minutes; the insides will finish cooking in the residual heat.

5 While the steak is cooking, place the butter, garlic and herbs in a small cast-iron pan on the barbecue. Heat until the butter is browned and has a nutty aroma, then remove from the heat and add the lemon juice (this will stop the butter cooking). Season with a little salt if needed.

6 Use a meat thermometer to check that the steak is ready to be moved off the barbecue: once inserted into the centre of the meat, it should register 45–48°C (the internal temperature will continue to rise as the meat rests). Transfer the meat to a warmed dish, pour on half of the browned butter and set aside to rest for 10–15 minutes.

7 Meanwhile, lay the asparagus spears on a small tray. Trickle over a couple of spoonfuls of browned butter and add a sprinkling of salt. Turn to coat well, then place the asparagus spears directly on the hot barbecue grid. Cook for around 5 minutes, turning them once or twice.

8 Once the steak has rested, carve it and serve with the baked potatoes and asparagus. As you dish up the steak, drizzle it with the nutty browned butter. Serve the blue cheese sauce on the side to spoon over the potatoes.

BARBECUED MEATBALL *and* MOZZARELLA SUB

serves **4**

Meatball subs are one of my all-time favourite sandwiches. Popular in the States but with Italian roots, these meatballs are made from beef, pork and Parmesan. The tomato barbecue sauce may not be traditional but it brings a bitter-sweet richness to my version of the classic.

. . . .

MEATBALLS

350g beef mince (15% fat)

150g sausage meat

2 rosemary sprigs, finely chopped

1 tsp onion powder

1 tsp garlic powder

30g Parmesan, finely grated

20g dried breadcrumbs

2 tbsp milk

Salt and freshly ground black pepper

TOMATO BARBECUE SAUCE

2 tbsp olive oil

4 garlic cloves, finely sliced

400ml passata

100ml barbecue sauce

50ml water

1 tsp dried chilli flakes

TO SERVE

4 sub rolls

2 tbsp butter, softened

200g scamorza or mozzarella, sliced

Basil leaves (optional)

Crispy fried onions, shop-bought (optional)

Hamburger pickles (optional)

1 To prepare the meatballs, put all the ingredients into a large bowl, seasoning well with salt and pepper, and mix well with your hands for a few minutes. Divide the mixture into 16 even-sized pieces and shape into balls. Place these balls on a tray and set aside.

2 To make the sauce, heat the olive oil in a cast-iron sauté pan on your hot barbecue. Add the garlic and stir well for 2 minutes. Add the passata, barbecue sauce, water and chilli flakes, season with salt and pepper and stir well. Cook for 10 minutes.

3 Meanwhile, place the meatballs directly on the hot barbecue grid and cook for around 5–8 minutes, turning regularly until browned all over. Lift the meatballs off the grid and add them to the sauce. Leave them to simmer and finish cooking in the sauce for 5–10 minutes.

4 To assemble, split the rolls open through the top and spread the cut surfaces with butter. Place 4 meatballs in each sub, spoon on some tomato barbecue sauce and top with cheese slices, and a few basil leaves if you like.

5 Wrap the rolls firmly in foil and place on the barbecue for 5–8 minutes, turning every minute or two to ensure even cooking. Remove from the barbecue and unwrap. Tuck some crispy onions and hamburger pickles into the subs for extra crunch.

...-inspired, spicy peanut mix that coats these beef
...f the most exciting flavour combinations in this book.
... won't be able to resist going back for more! Keep the
layer ... n the steak — it crisps up deliciously on the barbecue.

• •

500g sirloin steak

2 large garlic cloves, grated

2.5cm piece of fresh ginger, grated

1 tbsp Maggi liquid seasoning

4 tbsp vegetable oil

2 red peppers

2 green peppers

SUYA SPICE MIX

80g roasted peanuts, crushed

1 tbsp paprika

1 tbsp mild chilli powder (optional)

1 tbsp garlic salt

1 tbsp onion powder

1 tsp ground ginger

½ tsp ground cinnamon

½ tsp cracked black pepper

½ tsp salt

¼ tsp ground allspice

CABBAGE SALAD

350g white cabbage, finely shredded

1 red onion, finely sliced

4 spring onions, finely sliced

A large handful of parsley, chopped

3 tbsp extra virgin olive oil

Juice of 1 lime

Salt and freshly ground black pepper

TO SERVE

Lime wedges

1 First, prepare the suya spice mix: stir all the ingredients together in a small bowl until evenly mixed.

2 Cut the steak into 2.5cm pieces and place in a bowl. Add the garlic, ginger, Maggi seasoning, two-thirds of the suya spice and 2 tbsp of the oil. Mix together well, so that all the steak pieces are well coated.

3 Halve, core and deseed all the peppers, then cut them into 2.5cm pieces. Skewer the steak pieces onto 8 metal skewers, alternating them with the red and green pepper pieces. Leave to marinate for at least an hour, or in the fridge overnight.

4 To make the cabbage salad, put all the ingredients into a large bowl, seasoning with a little salt and pepper, and mix well.

5 When you are ready to cook them, brush the skewers lightly with the remaining 2 tbsp oil. Lay them on a medium-hot barbecue and cook for 12–15 minutes, turning every minute to ensure they cook evenly. The skewers should be lightly charred on all sides.

6 Serve the beef suya skewers on a platter with lime wedges for squeezing over and the cabbage salad alongside. Serve the remaining spice mix in a little dish on the side for guests to sprinkle over the skewers if they want to add an extra kick of spice.

T-BONE STEAK *with* BLACK PEPPER BUTTER

This is the king of steaks! Caramelised on the outside, juicy and tender on the inside, you can't beat a T-bone steak cooked on the barbecue. A colourful assortment of veg – cooked around the steak until tender and temptingly charred – is the perfect foil.

1 T-bone steak (about 900g), at room temperature

1 tbsp vegetable oil

1 tsp salt

BLACK PEPPER BUTTER

100g salted butter, softened

2 tsp cracked black pepper

1 tbsp Dijon mustard

A pinch of salt

CHARRED VEG

1 red onion, quartered

1 white onion, quartered

3–4 spring onions

1 medium leek (white part only), split lengthways and halved

6 tenderstem broccoli spears

1 lemon, cut in half

2 thyme sprigs

2 tbsp vegetable oil

Salt and freshly ground black pepper

1 First, prepare the black pepper butter: mix the ingredients together in a small bowl until evenly combined, then spoon onto the middle of a sheet of foil or cling film and roll to form a cylinder, roughly the diameter of a £1 coin. Twist the ends of the foil or cling film to seal and place in the fridge for 30 minutes to firm up.

2 Meanwhile, for the charred veg, place all the onions in a large bowl with the leek, broccoli, lemon and thyme. Drizzle with the oil and season with a little salt and pepper.

3 When ready to cook, rub the T-bone steak with the oil and salt, then lay on the hot barbecue grid and cook for 5 minutes. Using a pair of tongs, turn the steak over and cook for another 5 minutes.

4 Quickly place the onion wedges around the steak and cook, turning occasionally, for 5 minutes. Now lay the leek, spring onions, broccoli and lemon halves on the grid and scatter over the thyme sprigs. Cook until the veg are tender and charred on both sides, turning as necessary.

5 Once the steak is cooked, lift it off the barbecue onto a warmed platter. Cover the steak with an upturned bowl to keep it warm and leave to rest for 5–8 minutes. Meanwhile, unwrap the black pepper butter and slice into discs, the thickness of a £1 coin.

6 Carve the steak either side of the T-bone and place on a warmed platter or board. Lay the butter discs on top of the steak. Serve with the barbecued veggies and the charred lemons for squeezing over them.

SMOKY PASTRAMI BURGERS

serves 4

These burgers are inspired by the pastrami-filled Reuben sandwiches you find in New York delis. Pastrami is low in fat, but the suet keeps things nice and juicy on the grill. I also add a couple of handfuls of soaked wood chips to the coals to give the burgers extra smokiness.

Olive oil for cooking

2 large onions, diced

400g beef mince (15% fat)

50g beef suet

100g pastrami, torn to resemble pulled meat

2 garlic cloves, grated

Salt and freshly ground black pepper

SPICE CRUST

1 tbsp fennel seeds, toasted

1 tbsp coriander seeds, toasted

1 tbsp coarsely ground peppercorns

RUSSIAN DRESSING

100g mayonnaise

50g tomato ketchup

1 tbsp creamed horseradish

2 dashes of Worcestershire sauce

3 drops of Tabasco

Juice of ½ lemon

TO ASSEMBLE AND SERVE

4 slices of Emmenthal

4 ciabatta rolls, split

4 heaped tbsp sauerkraut

4 chunky dill pickles, halved lengthways

1 Heat a generous splash of olive oil in a large sauté pan. When hot, add the onions with a pinch of salt, stir and cook over a low to medium heat for about 20 minutes until soft and caramelised. Tip into a large bowl; leave to cool.

2 Add all the rest of the burger ingredients to the cooled onions, seasoning generously with salt and pepper. Mix thoroughly and bring the mixture together with your hands. Divide into 4 portions and flatten into patties. Lay on a tray, cover and place in the fridge for 1 hour to firm up.

3 For the spice crust, using a pestle and mortar, grind the spices to a coarse powder then tip onto a plate. Press one side of each pattie onto the spice mix to coat. Place the burgers, spice coated side up, on a tray, ready to cook.

4 To make the dressing, mix the ingredients together in a bowl and season with salt to taste; set aside.

5 Once your barbecue is hot, scatter a couple of handfuls of soaked wood chips onto the coals to create extra smoke. Lightly drizzle the burgers with oil, place spice side down on the barbecue and cook for 2 minutes. Flip the burgers over, lay the cheese on top and cook for a further 2–3 minutes. Remove to a warmed plate and leave to rest for a minute or two while you lightly toast the ciabatta rolls on the barbecue.

6 To assemble the burgers, spread the dressing on the roll bases and tops. Place a burger on each base and top with the sauerkraut and a dill pickle. Sandwich together with the tops of the rolls and tuck in straight away.

KOREAN BARBECUED BEEF

Korea is famous for its barbecue and this recipe is full of amazing Korean spices. Bavette steak is an inexpensive cut that cooks quickly; just keep an eye on it so it stays nice and pink inside. I serve it with kimchi, a kind of Korean-style slaw – spicy and without the mayo.

2 pieces of bavette steak (400g each)

MARINADE

4 tbsp gochujang paste

2 tbsp soy sauce (Kikkoman)

2 tsp caster sugar

2 tsp sesame oil

Salt and freshly ground white pepper

GINGER AND SPRING ONION DRESSING

80ml vegetable or groundnut oil

5cm piece of fresh ginger, finely grated

4 spring onions, finely sliced

2 tsp soy sauce (Kikkoman)

TO SERVE

300g sushi rice

300g kimchi

2 round or butterhead lettuce, leaves separated

Gochujang paste (optional)

Furikake seasoning (optional)

Crispy seaweed

1 For the marinade, put the gochujang paste, soy, sugar and sesame oil in a shallow tray with some salt and white pepper and mix well. Add the steaks and turn until well coated. Leave to marinate for at least 20 minutes.

2 Meanwhile, prepare the ginger and spring onion dressing. Heat the oil gently in a small cast-iron pan on the barbecue for 2–3 minutes or until warm. Test the heat by adding a little grated ginger to the oil; if it sizzles lightly it's ready. Remove the pan from the heat and add the ginger, spring onions and soy sauce. Mix well and leave to infuse.

3 Cook the sushi rice for serving in 420ml water; set aside, keeping it warm.

4 When you are ready to cook the steaks, make sure your barbecue is really hot. Lay the steaks on the barbecue and cook for 3–4 minutes on each side for medium to medium-rare. The timing will depend on the thickness of your steaks. You want the edges to get a little charred.

5 Lift the steaks off the barbecue onto a warm platter and leave to rest for 5 minutes. Meanwhile, place the cooked rice, kimchi, lettuce and any other condiments on the table. Slice the steak and serve in its resting juices.

6 To eat, place a little sushi rice in the middle of a lettuce leaf. Add some steak slices and kimchi then trickle over some ginger and spring onion dressing. Add a little gochujang paste or furikake seasoning if you like, and finish with some crispy seaweed. Enjoy!

LAMB RUMPS *with* HARISSA BUTTER

serves 4 – 6

Lamb chops are most people's go-to choice for the barbecue, but next time give lamb rump a go. It has loads more flavour! This recipe has a lovely North African feel, with the harissa flavouring in the butter and couscous salad on the side.

• •

2 lamb rumps (about 500g each)

2 tbsp extra virgin olive oil

Salt and freshly ground black pepper

HARISSA BUTTER

100g butter

1 tsp ground cumin

3 tsp rose harissa

COUSCOUS SALAD

800ml lamb stock

300g giant couscous

1 red onion, finely chopped

2 small cucumbers, finely chopped

80g pitted green olives, sliced

100g feta, crumbled

2 tbsp roughly chopped dill leaves

A large handful of parsley, roughly chopped

Juice of 1 lemon

2 tbsp pomegranate molasses

3 tbsp extra virgin olive oil

1 Using a sharp knife, score the fat side of each lamb rump in a criss-cross pattern. Rub both sides with olive oil and season with salt and pepper. Rub in well and leave to come up to room temperature.

2 For the harissa butter, put the ingredients into a small pan, add a little seasoning and place over a medium heat on the hob until the butter is melted. Set aside.

3 For the couscous salad, bring the stock to the boil in a pan and add the couscous. Bring back to a simmer and cook for 10 minutes or so, until all the liquid is absorbed and the couscous is tender. Remove from the heat and let cool slightly.

4 When you are ready to cook the lamb, place the rumps over a medium-high heat on the barbecue and sear for 1 minute on each side. Now move them to a medium heat and start basting with the harissa butter. Cook for around 8 minutes on each side until well coloured. Check the cooking with a meat thermometer – once inserted into the middle of a rump, it should register 50–55°C. Remove to a tray and pour over any remaining harissa butter. Rest for 5 minutes or so.

5 Meanwhile, add all the remaining salad ingredients to the couscous and toss gently. Season with salt and pepper to taste.

6 Carve the lamb rumps into thick slices and serve with the resting juices and any remaining butter trickled over. Serve the couscous salad alongside.

LAMB KOFTAS

I love cooking lamb mince on the grill. It's quite high in fat so the koftas won't dry out and they crisp up wonderfully on the surface. Lamb can take on as much flavour and heat as you want, so don't be afraid to go big on the spicing. Lemon zest and mint sauce cut through the richness.

A splash of vegetable oil

1 onion, diced

1 tsp cumin seeds, toasted

1 tsp coriander seeds

2 tsp cracked black pepper

2 tsp salt

800g lamb belly, minced

4 garlic cloves, finely grated

1 tsp ras el hanout

1 tsp ready-made mint sauce

Finely grated zest of 1 lemon

2 tbsp chopped parsley

1 tbsp chopped coriander

TO SERVE

Lemon wedges

Coriander leaves

Spicy fennel and pomegranate slaw
  (page 211)

1 Heat the oil in a frying pan on the hob and fry the diced onion over a medium heat for 8–10 minutes until soft. Take off the heat and leave to cool. Meanwhile, using a pestle and mortar, grind the spices and salt together until you have a fine spice mix.

2 Put the lamb mince into a large bowl with the cooled onion, garlic, ground spice mix, ras el hanout, mint sauce, lemon zest and herbs. Mix well with your hands.

3 Divide the mixture into 8 equal portions and roll each into a sausage-shaped kofta. Lay them on a lined tray and chill in the fridge for 1 hour, to firm up.

4 When you are ready to cook the koftas, take them from the fridge. Place on the edges of your hot barbecue to achieve a medium heat – as these koftas tend to release some fat, it's best not to have them over a direct flame. Cook for around 8 minutes, turning regularly.

5 Once cooked, serve the lamb koftas on a platter with lemon wedges. Garnish with coriander and serve the fennel and pomegranate slaw alongside.

THE ULTIMATE HOT DOG

serves **4**

These hot dogs are based on everyone's favourite Christmas side: pigs in blankets. Like Christmas trees, hot dogs are thought to originate in Germany, so I've added a bit of curry powder, German mustard and Bavarian cheese as a nod to that. Great to cook outside on a cold day!

BARBECUE BURNT ONIONS

2 large onions, finely sliced

3 tbsp vegetable oil

PIGS IN BLANKETS

4 jumbo sausages

2 heaped tsp mild curry powder

12 rashers of streaky bacon

GERMAN MUSTARD MAYO

100g thick mayonnaise

40g German mustard

3 tsp finely chopped shallot

10 cornichons, finely sliced

2 tbsp finely chopped dill

Salt and freshly ground black pepper

TO ASSEMBLE

4 long hot dog rolls

8 thick slices of smoked Bavarian cheese

8 large slices of dill pickle

A bunch of spring onions, green part only, finely sliced

1 To cook the onions, place a cast-iron pan on the hot barbecue and add the oil. When it is hot, add the onions with a generous pinch of salt. Stir well and cook for about 20 minutes until softened, dark and caramelised.

2 Meanwhile, prepare the sausages. Poke a metal skewer through the length of each sausage and lay the skewers on a tray. Season with the curry powder, trying to get an even coating all over the sausages. Wrap each one in bacon, using 3 rashers per sausage, and secure the bacon with a couple of cocktail sticks.

3 Lay the bacon-wrapped sausages on the hot barbecue and cook for about 10 minutes, turning every minute or two. While they are on the barbecue, mix the German mustard mayo ingredients together in a bowl, seasoning with salt and pepper to taste; set aside until needed.

4 Once the sausages are cooked through, lift them off the barbecue and place on a tray. Remove the cocktail sticks and metal skewers.

5 To build the hot dogs, slit the rolls open through the top and lay the cheese slices in them. Add the bacon-wrapped sausages and top with plenty of caramelised onions and the pickle slices.

6 Place the hot dogs on a sturdy baking tray on the barbecue, put the lid on and leave for a minute or two so that the cheese becomes all gooey and melted. Transfer the hot dogs to plates and spoon on the German mayo. Scatter over the spring onions for freshness and serve.

PORK RIBS *with* YELLOW BARBECUE SAUCE

serves 4

Full of big strong, Deep South-style flavours, these ribs are irresistible. The sauce caramelises beautifully on the ribs as they cook, without being overly sweet. Steaming the ribs in beer at the start is what will give you meat that falls off the bone – the ultimate in barbecue goals.

2 racks of baby back pork ribs, trimmed and cleaned of all sinew

330ml can beer

SPICE RUB

2 tsp table salt

2 tbsp smoked paprika

2 tsp garlic powder

4 tbsp vegetable oil

1 tbsp maple syrup

YELLOW BARBECUE SAUCE

100ml American mustard

2 tbsp runny honey

1 tbsp bourbon

2 tbsp cider vinegar

2 tbsp soft light brown sugar

TO SERVE

Fennel and cabbage slaw (page 211)

1 For the spice rub, mix all the ingredients together in a small bowl. Lay the rib racks in a large roasting dish and massage all over with the spice rub.

2 Pour the beer into the dish then cover with foil (this will help the ribs steam while they bake in the covered barbecue). If you have time, leave to marinate for an hour or so (bring back to room temperature before cooking if you do this in the fridge).

3 If you have a temperature-controlled barbecue, cook the dish of ribs in it with the convector plate fitted at 150°C (alternatively use a conventional oven at 150°C/ Fan 130°C/Gas 2), for 2 hours. Once cooked, remove the ribs from the barbecue and leave to cool slightly.

4 In the meantime, make the sauce: put the mustard, honey, bourbon, cider vinegar and brown sugar into a saucepan over a medium heat and stir to dissolve the sugar. Bring to the boil, then take off the heat; set aside.

5 When ready to eat, lay the ribs on your hot barbecue and colour them for a minute or two on each side. Now, using a pastry brush, glaze the ribs with the yellow mustard sauce and cook them for a further 2–3 minutes. Once the sugar starts to caramelise, brush them again and barbecue for a few more minutes until you have lovely glazed ribs.

6 Transfer the ribs to a serving platter and serve the fennel and cabbage slaw alongside. If you have any of the yellow barbecue sauce left, serve it as a dipping sauce for the ribs.

JERK PORK *and* PINEAPPLE SKEWERS

makes **8**

Jerk seasoning and pineapple are the perfect pairing on a skewer. This is a cooking process to relax into and enjoy – be sure to give your pork enough time to marinate and don't rush the barbecue. You could buy a ready-made jerk paste, but the flavours in this version are incredible.

1kg pork shoulder, cut into 2.5cm pieces

500g fresh pineapple, peeled, cored and cut into 2.5cm pieces

Sea salt and freshly ground black pepper

JERK SEASONING PASTE

4 spring onions, trimmed and roughly chopped

2 large garlic cloves, roughly chopped

A 2.5cm piece of fresh ginger, roughly chopped

1 large habanero chilli, chopped (seeds retained)

2 tbsp thyme leaves

2 tbsp soft light brown sugar

2 tbsp soy sauce (Kikkoman)

3 tbsp vegetable oil

2 tsp ground allspice

1 tsp ground turmeric

Juice of 1 lime

TO SERVE

Coriander leaves

Hot sauce

Lime wedges

Roti bread

1 First make the jerk seasoning paste. Put all the ingredients into a small food processor or jug blender and blend to a smooth paste.

2 Place the pork in a bowl, add the jerk paste and mix well until all the pieces are evenly coated. Cover with cling film and leave to marinate for at least an hour.

3 Add 1 tsp sea salt and several grindings of pepper to the marinating pork and mix again. Thread the pork and pineapple onto 8 metal skewers, alternating them.

4 Lay the skewers on a medium-hot barbecue and cook for around 15 minutes, turning every 2 minutes or so – to ensure they char evenly all over.

5 Transfer the skewers to a warmed plate, sprinkle with coriander and add a bit of your favourite hot sauce. Serve hot, with lime wedges for squeezing and warm roti bread alongside.

TIP

Habanero chillies are super-hot, so feel free to adjust the amount in the jerk seasoning according to the level of chilli heat you like.

PORK BÁNH MÌ

This is a bit like a Vietnamese-style hot dog. The liver pâté in the baguette might be an unexpected addition, but it provides a savoury depth that really enhances the flavour of the pork. The sticky marinade brings the sweetness, while my quick pickle gives it a fresh lift.

• •

2 pork loins, about 400g each

MARINADE

2 tbsp lemongrass paste

2 tsp caster sugar

4 tbsp fish sauce

4 tbsp soy sauce (Kikkoman)

2 large garlic cloves, finely grated

½ tsp dried chilli flakes

PICKLE

250ml rice vinegar

100ml water

2 tbsp caster sugar

1 tbsp sea salt flakes

100g carrot, julienned

6 radishes, halved and thinly sliced

100g cucumber, julienned

1 long red chilli, thinly sliced on
   an angle

TO ASSEMBLE

4 long hot dog rolls

100g chicken liver pâté

6 tbsp Japanese mayo (or use 6 tbsp
   classic mayonnaise mixed with 1 tbsp
   rice wine vinegar and ½ tsp sugar)

4 tbsp crispy onions (shop-bought)

A large handful of coriander leaves

1 Trim the pork of any sinew and then cut each loin in half so you have 4 pieces, each about 14cm long.

2 For the marinade, mix the ingredients together in a shallow dish (that will hold the pork snugly). Add the pork and turn to coat well. Leave to marinate for 20 minutes, turning the meat over halfway through.

3 For the pickle liquor, put the rice vinegar, water, sugar and salt into a pan over a medium heat on the hob and stir to dissolve the sugar. Take off the heat; leave to cool.

4 Place the carrot, radishes, cucumber and chilli in a small bowl and toss to mix. Pour the cooled pickling liquor over the veg and leave for at least 15 minutes to pickle. Before serving, drain and tip into a bowl.

5 When you are ready to cook, lift the pork out of the dish and place on a medium-hot barbecue. Cook for around 12–15 minutes, turning regularly and basting with the residual marinade. The pork should be slightly springy to the touch and lightly charred all over. Remove to a plate, cover with foil and leave to rest for 10 minutes.

6 To assemble your bánh mì, cut the rolls through the middle. Spread a thick layer of chicken liver pâté on the bottom and a thick layer of Japanese mayo on the top of each roll. Cut the pork into 5mm thick slices and lay them on the pâté. Distribute a handful of pickled veg over the pork slices and scatter with crispy onions and coriander leaves. Sandwich together and serve straight away.

FENNEL *and* 'NDUJA SPICED PORCHETTA

FENNEL *and* 'NDUJA SPICED PORCHETTA

serves **6 – 8**

You need to start this recipe a day ahead but it's worth it, because the flavours are unbelievable, and it makes a great barbecue centrepiece. I like to serve the porchetta with a big green salad and baked potatoes, which you can cook on the barbecue.

3kg belly of pork, boned and skin scored (ask your butcher to do this)

FENNEL AND 'NDUJA STUFFING

2 tbsp vegetable oil

2 onions, diced

½ fennel bulb, diced (to the same size as the onion)

3 garlic cloves, coarsely chopped

100g pine nuts, toasted

100g pitted green olives, sliced

175g 'nduja (spicy spreadable sausage)

FENNEL AND SAGE SEASONING

3 tsp salt

50g fennel seeds

25g cracked black pepper

10 sage leaves

1 First, make the fennel and 'nduja stuffing. Place a large frying pan over a medium heat on the hob and add the oil. Once it is hot, add the diced onions and fennel and fry for about 10 minutes until softened and golden brown, adding the garlic after about 5 minutes. Stir in the pine nuts, olives and 'nduja and warm through briefly. Spoon the stuffing onto a tray, spread out and leave to cool.

2 Lay the belly of pork skin side down on a board then butterfly, using a sharp knife: cut through horizontally from one long side almost to the other, so you leave that end intact; be careful not to slice all the way through. Now open up the belly.

3 For the fennel and sage seasoning, mix the salt, fennel seeds and cracked pepper together in a bowl.

4 Sprinkle the seasoning evenly over the butterflied pork belly and scatter the sage leaves on top, distributing them evenly. Fold the belly to enclose. Cover and place in the fridge to chill for an hour.

5 Lay the pork belly back on the board and open it up again to expose the seasoned side. Spread the stuffing evenly over the surface, using a palette knife or the back of a spoon, leaving a margin at the edges.

6 Now roll the meat up tightly and tie with kitchen string at roughly 4cm intervals, starting in the middle and working out towards the ends. It should be firmly tied, but not so tight that the filling is squeezed out. Place the porchetta on a tray in the fridge overnight. >

7 The next day, remove the pork from the fridge at least an hour before you intend to start cooking it.

8 If you have a temperature-controlled barbecue, fit the convector plate and heat to 160°C. Place the meat on the convector plate and close the lid. Roast for 4½ hours until meltingly tender. (If you do not have a temperature-controlled barbecue, cook the pork on a baking tray in a conventional oven at 160°C/Fan 140°C/Gas 3 for 3½ hours and finish over a moderate heat on the barbecue with the lid on for the final hour, turning from time to time.)

9 Once the porchetta is cooked, lift it off the barbecue, transfer to a warmed platter and leave to rest for 15–20 minutes. Carve the meat into thick slices and serve with your chosen accompaniments.

TIP

If you're serving baked jacket potatoes with the porchetta, rub 6–8 large baking potatoes all over with oil and season with salt and dried oregano, then wrap in foil. Barbecue alongside the pork for the final 1¼ hours of the cooking time, turning from time to time, until the flesh is soft. Open up the foil for the last 20 minutes or so to crisp the skins.

SPICY PORK BURGERS *with* ROMANESCO SALSA

serves 4

Everyone loves a burger on the barbecue, and it's a great chance to get creative and try something new. This Spanish-inspired pork burger is topped with smoky Romanesco salsa instead of ketchup, and slices of Manchego cheese. Quick pickled onions add a burst of acidity.

• •

A splash of vegetable oil, plus extra to brush

1 large onion

400g minced pork shoulder

175g soft cooking chorizo sausages, skin removed, broken into small pieces

1 red chilli, deseeded and finely diced

3 garlic cloves, grated

½ tsp cumin seeds, toasted and ground to a powder

½ tsp ground coriander

1 tsp smoked paprika

25g medium polenta

½ tsp bicarbonate of soda

1 tsp thyme leaves

A little melted butter to brush

Salt and freshly ground black pepper

ROMANESCO SALSA

3 red peppers

2 tomatoes, skinned, quartered and deseeded

70g blanched almonds, toasted

30g dried breadcrumbs, toasted

½ tsp dried chilli flakes

1 tbsp chopped parsley

Finely grated zest of 1 lemon

100ml extra virgin olive oil

Ingredients continue >

1 Prepare the pickled red onions an hour or so ahead (ingredients listed overleaf). Put the onions into a small heatproof bowl. Combine the cider vinegar, sugar, mustard seeds and star anise in a small pan. Place over a medium heat on the hob to dissolve the sugar and bring to the boil. Immediately pour over the sliced onion and leave to cool. Once cooled, stir in the dill.

2 To prepare the burgers, heat the oil in a small pan, add the onion and fry gently for about 15 minutes until soft and caramelised. Tip into a large bowl and allow to cool.

3 Add the minced pork, chorizo, chilli, garlic and ground spices to the fried onion. Add the polenta, bicarbonate of soda, thyme and some salt and pepper. Mix thoroughly, bringing the mixture together with your hands.

4 Divide the burger mixture into 4 portions and flatten into patties. Lay on a tray, cover with cling film and place in the fridge to firm up for at least an hour.

5 For the salsa, place the peppers on the hot barbecue and cook, turning carefully, until the skin starts to blister and char; this will give the salsa a lovely smoky finish. Lift off the barbecue, place in a bowl and cover tightly with cling film. Allow to steam in the bowl for 5–10 minutes, then lift out. Peel away the skins from the peppers and remove the seeds; discard any juices. Cut the peppers and into 5mm dice and place in a bowl. Cut the tomatoes into similar-sized dice and add to the peppers. >

PICKLED RED ONIONS

2 medium red onions, sliced into
5mm rings

200ml cider vinegar

60g demerara sugar

1 tbsp mustard seeds, toasted

1 star anise

1 tbsp dill leaves

TO ASSEMBLE AND SERVE

4 slices of Manchego cheese

8 Padrón peppers

Extra olive oil to drizzle

4 brioche burger buns, split

8 slices of Serrano ham

Flaky sea salt

6 Roughly chop the toasted nuts and add to the peppers and tomatoes with the toasted breadcrumbs, chilli flakes, chopped parsley, lemon zest, extra virgin olive oil and some salt and pepper. Toss to mix and taste to check the seasoning.

7 Make sure the barbecue is good and hot before you cook the burgers. Take the patties from the fridge and brush each side with a little oil. Lay them on the hot barbecue and cook for 3–4 minutes until nicely charred on the underside. Flip the burgers over and repeat to char the other side. Turn the burgers over once more, brush with a little melted butter and cook for a further 2–3 minutes. Lay the Manchego slices on the burgers.

8 Dress the Padrón peppers with oil and salt and throw them onto the hot barbecue to cook for a couple of minutes. Lift off the peppers and thread a couple onto each of 4 short wooden skewers. Lightly toast the brioche buns on the barbecue.

9 To assemble your burgers, place a cooked burger on the bottom half of each toasted brioche bun. Spoon on some Romanesco salsa then top with pickled red onion and a couple of Serrano ham slices. Sandwich together with the brioche bun tops and skewer with the Padrón pepper skewers to hold the burgers in place. Serve at once.

Fish

FEISTY

FRAGRANT

FRESH

FISH

· ·

Simply grilled fish and seafood are a real taste of summer holidays. They conjure up images of fishermen coming in with their morning haul on a beautiful sunny beach in Greece or Italy, or eating freshly cooked seafood in a beach-side taverna. The recipes in this chapter will help recreate some of those great holiday memories in your own back garden.

Fish needs to be treated a bit gently when it comes to adding flavour. It's not as robust as beef or chicken and it doesn't take as long to cook, so you don't need to wrap it in flavours in the same way. Think lighter, fresher, subtle flavours, rather than heady, deep, bold spices. Both fish and seafood take on the smokiness from the grill brilliantly, and just a drizzle of olive oil and some fresh herbs or lemon are often all you need.

The same applies when it comes to thinking about what sides to pair your fish with – go for lighter dishes, such as the warm courgette, feta and herb salad on page 192 rather than the spicy charred cauliflower salad on page 197. You don't want the sides to overpower the fish. Keep thinking of that beach barbecue in Greece and you won't go wrong!

Shellfish are a fantastic addition to the barbecue. They turn barbecue cooking into a real event, and are surprisingly easy to cook, especially as some of them – prawns, scallops, langoustines, clams – come in their own protective cases. And nothing looks more impressive or feels more luxurious than a seafood platter like the one on page 102.

I know you're worried about fish sticking to the barbecue, and it's true that this can happen – but there are a few ways you can reduce the chances. The first is to think about the type of fish you use. Go for a meaty species like sea bass or monkfish and fish with thick skins, or oily fish like mackerel or sardines. Tuna is another great fish to cook on the barbecue. You can get a thick piece and cook it just like a steak – I like to sear it on both sides and keep it almost raw in the middle, as in the tuna tacos on page 118. Another way to avoid the issue of sticking is to use big pieces of fish on skewers, as for the tandoori fish skewers on page 122.

Don't be afraid of putting whole fish on the barbecue either. They hold their shape and keep lovely and moist. I use a fish cage (also called a fish basket) for whole fish. This may sound a bit cheffy but it's such a useful item of kit; it looks impressive too! You can pack it with herbs and aromatics to lend extra flavour and it's easy to turn on the grill.

Try the sea bass with sauce vierge on page 110 or the whole bream with smoked potato salad on page 117. Who says barbecuing can't be restaurant quality?

Don't be afraid to use the barbecue like a hob too. You can pan-fry your fish either on the grill rack or directly on the coals, which means you have more control, while still getting in that amazing smoky taste.

There are few things more summery than barbecued fish and seafood. Whether that's juicy prawns wrapped in foil as on page 105 or you go all out with the lobster thermidor on page 106, your barbecue will always be a meal to remember.

SEAFOOD PLATTER

Cooking shellfish on the barbecue looks hugely impressive but it is actually very simple. The buttery scallops and oysters cook in their shells, which act like little dishes so they keep lovely and tender. This platter, with its three flavoured butters, is a real summer showstopper.

4 medium squid with tentacles, cleaned

A splash of olive oil

4 scallops, cleaned, in their half-shells

6 oysters, cleaned, in their half-shells

8 razor clams

8–12 large raw red prawns

300g samphire, blanched

Salt and freshly ground black pepper

'NDUJA BUTTER

100g salted butter

½ tsp smoked paprika

2 tbsp 'nduja paste

SEAWEED BUTTER

100g salted butter, at room temperature

1 tbsp dried nori seaweed flakes

2 tsp crushed pink peppercorns

1 tsp crushed fennel seeds

LEMONGRASS AND CHILLI BUTTER

100g salted butter, at room temperature

1 bird's eye red chilli, finely chopped

1 garlic clove, grated

1 tsp lemongrass paste

1 tsp fish sauce

2 tbsp chopped coriander

TO SERVE

2 lemons, cut into wedges

Crusty bread

1 First, prepare the flavoured butters. For the 'nduja butter, put the ingredients into a small cast-iron saucepan, place on the barbecue and cook for a few minutes.

2 For the seaweed butter, mix all the ingredients together in a bowl until evenly blended. Do the same to make the lemongrass and chilli butter. Cover and set aside.

3 To prepare the squid, lay them on a board and cut in half lengthways. Score a lattice pattern on the softer, internal surface with a sharp knife. Trim any long tentacles. Lay the squid pieces and tentacles on a tray. Drizzle with a little olive oil and sprinkle with salt and pepper, then turn them over and do the same thing on the other side.

4 When you are ready to cook, assemble all the shellfish by the barbecue. Add a little seaweed or lemongrass and chilli butter to the scallops and oysters to flavour them while they are cooking. Place the scallops and oysters (in their shells) on the barbecue grid. After about a minute, lay the razor clams and prawns on the grid. After another minute add the squid, laying the pieces and tentacles directly on the grid, and cook for 1–2 minutes, no longer. As they cook, brush them with your favourite butter.

5 Once each item is cooked, transfer it to a tray and keep warm near the barbecue. Scatter the blanched samphire over your serving platter and lay all your cooked seafood on top. Spoon any leftover butters into small dishes and serve alongside the seafood so people can add more themselves. Serve with lemon wedges for squeezing, and hot crusty bread.

SMOKY PRAWNS COOKED IN FOIL

serves 4

This no-hassle, no-mess dish is perfect for prepping ahead and sticking on the barbie as everyone arrives. The prawns steam-cook wrapped in foil, which locks in moisture to keep them juicy. Get people round the table as you undo the parcel – to savour the incredible garlicky aroma.

600g large raw tiger prawns

100g butter

4 tbsp extra virgin olive oil

5 garlic cloves, thinly sliced

1 long red chilli, sliced

1 tsp sweet smoked paprika

80ml dry sherry

Salt and freshly ground pepper

TO FINISH AND SERVE

2 tbsp roughly chopped flat-leaf parsley

Crusty bread

1 First, peel the prawns, removing the heads but leaving the tail shells on. Using a sharp knife, make a small slit along the middle of the back to expose the dark intestinal vein. Prise this out with the tip of your knife and discard it.

2 Tear off a 45cm length of foil and place shiny side down on your work surface. Fold the foil in half, then create a pocket by sealing the sides (to do this, fold the foil edges over and over a few times, pressing firmly). Put the prawns into the foil pocket through the opening at the top.

3 Put the butter, olive oil, garlic, chilli, smoked paprika and sherry into a small pan. Place over a high heat and let it bubble away for 2 minutes. Take off the heat and season well with salt and pepper.

4 Pour the butter over the prawns in the foil pocket. Fold the foil edges together along the open side to seal the parcel completely. Place the foil parcel on your hot barbecue and cook for 12–15 minutes, depending on the heat. You'll be able to tell that it's nearly ready when the envelope begins to puff up with steam.

5 Remove the foil parcel from the barbecue, open it up carefully and tip the prawns and buttery juices into a serving bowl then sprinkle with chopped parsley – or just rip it open, throw in the parsley and tuck in! Make sure there's lots of crusty bread around to dunk in the juices.

TIP

Instead of a foil parcel, you can cook the prawns in a sealed rigid foil container – for better stability.

Fish · 105

LOBSTER THERMIDOR

serves 2 as a main or 4 as a starter

A truly luxury dish for a special occasion. Yes, you'll need to spend a bit of money on it, but the flavours in this classic dish are unbeatable. Rich, herby, slightly spicy butter is brushed on as the lobster cooks, making for a super-indulgent barbecue feast to remember.

● ●

2 native lobsters (about 700g each), split in half

THERMIDOR BUTTER

150g butter, slightly softened

1 large banana shallot, finely diced

1 tbsp chopped chives

1 tbsp chopped chervil

1 tbsp chopped parsley

1 tbsp Dijon mustard

Finely grated zest of 1 lemon

70g Parmesan, freshly grated

1 egg yolk

½ tsp cayenne pepper

A pinch of salt

TO SERVE

Mixed leaf salad

Lemon wedges

Crusty bread

1 To prepare the thermidor butter, put all of the ingredients into a bowl and beat until fully combined.

2 Lay the lobster halves on a board and lightly tap the claws with the back of your knife to crack them open – this will help the claw meat to cook as quickly as the tail meat in the middle.

3 Place the lobster halves, cut side up, on a metal tray and spoon the thermidor butter evenly over the flesh. Place the tray on the barbecue, put the lid on and cook for 12–15 minutes or so, or until the lobster meat is cooked.

4 Carefully transfer the lobster halves to individual plates and pile some salad leaves on the side. Serve with lemon wedges on the side for squeezing over, and some crusty bread to soak up all the buttery lobster juices.

SQUID, CHORIZO and CHICKPEA SALAD

serves **6**

This is a fantastic Spanish-style dish: smoky spicy chorizo, dressed chickpeas and veg, and crisp garlic croûtons. Squid has a subtle taste and great texture that responds well to flame-cooking. Don't worry if it sticks to the grill in places, you'll just have more sticky caramelised bits.

1kg cleaned squid with tentacles

2 tsp sweet smoked paprika

2 large garlic cloves, finely grated

Finely grated zest and juice of 1 lemon

7 tbsp extra virgin olive oil

2 x 400g tins chickpeas, drained and rinsed

300g courgettes, diced

350g baby plum or cherry tomatoes, halved

2 tbsp sherry vinegar

4 cooking chorizo sausages, halved lengthways

A handful of flat-leaf parsley leaves, roughly chopped

Salt and freshly ground black pepper

GARLIC TOASTS

50g butter, softened

1 large garlic clove, finely grated

1 tbsp finely chopped flat-leaf parsley

4 slices of sourdough

1 To prepare the squid, lay them on a board and cut in half lengthways. Score a lattice pattern on the softer, internal surface with a sharp knife. Trim any long tentacles. Put all the squid into a bowl and add the smoked paprika, garlic, lemon zest and 3 tbsp olive oil. Season well with salt and pepper. Mix well and leave to marinate for 20 minutes.

2 Meanwhile, tip the chickpeas into a large shallow bowl and add the diced courgettes and baby tomatoes. Add the lemon juice, sherry vinegar and remaining 4 tbsp olive oil. Season with salt and pepper, and toss to mix.

3 For the garlic toasts, in a small bowl, mix the butter with the garlic and parsley until evenly combined. Spread both sides of the sourdough with the garlic butter.

4 When you're ready, lay the chorizo sausages on the hot barbecue. Add the sourdough slices too – slightly away from the coals as the butter may drip. Cook the chorizo for 3–4 minutes on each side. The toast is ready when it is golden brown on both sides. Remove and set aside on a warmed platter while you cook the squid.

5 Place the squid scored side down on the hot barbecue, along with the tentacles, and cook for 2–3 minutes. Turn and repeat to cook the other side.

6 As soon as it is cooked, remove the squid from the barbecue and cut into bite-sized pieces. Do the same with the chorizo and garlic toast. Add the squid, chorizo and garlic toast to the chickpea salad, along with the chopped parsley. Toss gently and serve.

SEA BASS *with* SAUCE VIERGE

Sauce vierge is a warm summer salsa from the south of France.
It was one of the first sauces I learnt to make when I was training
as a chef and it goes brilliantly with fish. Sea bass is a good option
for the barbecue as it's robust and holds its shape well in a fish cage.

. . . .

1 large sea bass (1.6–2kg), descaled
and gutted

6 rosemary sprigs

1 small lemon, sliced (ends discarded)

40ml olive oil

Flaky sea salt and freshly ground
pepper

SAUCE VIERGE

4 plum tomatoes, skinned

100ml extra virgin olive oil

1 tsp coriander seeds, toasted and
lightly crushed

2 garlic cloves, grated

Finely grated zest and juice of ½ lemon

8 pitted black olives, finely chopped

1 tbsp finely chopped flat-leaf parsley

1 tbsp finely chopped basil leaves

GRILLED BROCCOLI

250g purple sprouting broccoli

2 tbsp olive oil

4 anchovy fillets in oil, drained
and chopped

1 To prepare the sea bass, cut off the fins with sharp
scissors and slice off the head with a sharp knife. Put a
couple of rosemary sprigs on one side of your fish cage.
Place the sea bass on top and tuck a couple of rosemary
sprigs and the lemon slices into the fish cavity. Lay the rest
of the rosemary sprigs on top of the sea bass and close
the fish cage.

2 When you're ready to cook, drizzle both sides of the
fish with olive oil and sprinkle with flaky salt. Place the
fish cage over a medium heat on the barbecue. Cook for
8–10 minutes, then turn the cage over and cook the fish
on the other side for the same time. The herbs will scorch
and impart a slight smoky herb flavour to the fish; the
lemon will char and create a lovely flavourful steam.

3 While your fish is cooking, make the sauce. Halve and
deseed the tomatoes then cut into 5mm dice and place
in a bowl. In a small saucepan over a medium-low heat on
the barbecue, warm the olive oil together with the crushed
coriander seeds for about 5 minutes. Add the garlic, give
it a stir, then remove from the heat and let cool slightly for
a few minutes.

4 Pour the coriander-infused oil over the tomatoes and
add the lemon zest and juice, olives and chopped
herbs. Season with salt and pepper to taste.

5 Once the sea bass is cooked, remove the cage from the
barbecue and rest the fish on a tray for a few minutes. ›

6 Meanwhile, drizzle the broccoli with olive oil and season with a little flaky salt. Lay the broccoli directly on the barbecue grid and cook for 3–4 minutes, turning to cook evenly. Transfer to a warmed bowl, add the anchovies and toss to mix.

7 Take the sea bass out of the fish cage and transfer it to a warm serving platter, discarding the charred herbs. Spoon some of the sauce vierge over the fish and spoon the rest into a serving bowl. Bring the fish to the table along with the grilled broccoli and sauce vierge, so everyone can help themselves.

SPICED MONKFISH *with* YOGHURT DRESSING

serves **4**

Monkfish is chunky and you can treat it a bit like a steak, so it's a great choice if you're a bit nervous about cooking fish. It handles spice really well, as in this bold, Indian-style dish. You'll find the salad has a lovely, fruity acidity from the chaat masala, which contains mango powder.

2 prepared monkfish tails (500g each)

3 tbsp vegetable oil

1 tbsp sea salt

2 tbsp Madras curry powder

1 tsp ground turmeric

100g salted butter, melted

½ lemon

KACHUMBER SALAD

2 cucumbers, deseeded and diced

1 small red onion, diced

150g cherry tomatoes, quartered

A good squeeze of lemon juice

A handful of mint leaves, chopped

A pinch of salt

1 tsp chaat masala

2 tbsp light olive oil

YOGHURT DRESSING

200ml natural yoghurt

½ tsp ground cumin

¼ tsp cayenne pepper

¼ tsp ground turmeric

A good squeeze of lemon juice

TO SERVE

2 limes, cut in half

1 Lay the monkfish tails on a large tray. Mix the oil, salt, curry powder and turmeric together in a bowl. Brush this seasoning all over the monkfish. Pop the fish into the fridge for an hour to marinate, if you've got the time.

2 When you're ready to cook, lay the fish down on your hot barbecue across the grid, so that you'll get chargrill lines. Cook for 2–3 minutes on each side or until the spices begin to caramelise.

3 Brush a little of the melted butter over each monkfish tail and cook for a further 6–8 minutes, turning the fish constantly so that it cooks evenly; it will take on a lovely smoky flavour.

4 While the fish is cooking, put all the ingredients for the kachumber salad into a large bowl, toss to combine and set aside.

5 Whisk the ingredients for the yoghurt dressing together in a bowl until evenly combined.

6 Once cooked, remove the monkfish from the barbecue and place on a warmed serving dish. Brush with any remaining butter and squeeze over the lemon juice then leave to rest for a few minutes.

7 Serve the monkfish with the kachumber salad, yoghurt dressing and lime halves on the side, for squeezing over the fish.

WHOLE BREAM *with* SMOKED POTATO SALAD

serves 2 (generously)

Bream holds it shape on the grill and the flavours in this spice rub are incredible – rosemary, fennel seeds, garlic and paprika. The smells coming off your barbecue will bring all the neighbours round! The potato salad served alongside goes well with grilled meats too.

2 bream or John Dory (500g each), gutted, fins and sharp spikes removed

Juice of 1 lemon

RUB

3 rosemary sprigs, leaves finely chopped

4 tbsp olive oil

1 tbsp flaky sea salt

1 tsp smoked paprika

2 tsp fennel seeds, lightly ground

1½ tsp garlic powder

SMOKED POTATO SALAD

800g cooked new potatoes, halved

3 tbsp good-quality mayonnaise

3 tbsp thick crème fraîche

6 celery sticks, finely chopped

50g cornichons, sliced

2 tbsp dill, roughly chopped

2 tbsp finely chopped flat-leaf parsley

Salt and freshly ground black pepper

1 Lay the fish on a board and make several slashes through the skin on each side at even intervals – to allow the fish to cook more quickly and encourage the skin to crisp up.

2 For the spice rub, put all the ingredients into a shallow tray that will hold the fish, and mix with a spoon. Lay the fish on the spice rub and massage it all over the fish, making sure you work it into those cuts.

3 When you're ready to cook, lay the fish directly on the hot barbecue and leave for 5–6 minutes until the skin crisps up and blisters – charred fish skin is deliciously slightly sweet, savoury and crispy. Carefully turn the fish over and repeat on the other side.

4 Once it is cooked, carefully lift the fish off the barbecue and place it on a tray. Squeeze over the lemon juice and leave to rest for 3 minutes.

5 If you have barbecue wood chips to hand, scatter some onto the barbecue and wait a minute or so, until they start smoking. Pop your precooked potatoes into a colander on the barbecue, put the lid on and leave them to smoke for 3–4 minutes. If you don't have any wood chips, cook the potatoes directly on the cooling embers.

6 Meanwhile, in a large bowl, mix together all the other ingredients for the potato salad, seasoning with salt and pepper to taste. Add the smoked potatoes and toss well to coat evenly.

7 Serve the barbecued fish with the warm smoked potato salad alongside.

TUNA TACOS *with* PINEAPPLE SALSA

serves 4

With lots of punchy flavours and contrasting textures working together in every bite, fish tacos are the perfect, light sharing meal. I like to keep the tuna quite rare – just searing it on either side – but cook it for longer if you prefer. Set everything out and let people assemble their own.

400g fresh tuna steaks, about 3cm thick
1 tsp dried chipotle chilli flakes
½ tsp dried oregano
Finely grated zest of 1 lime
2 tbsp extra virgin olive oil
Salt

PICKLED RADISHES

12 radishes, thinly sliced
Juice of 1 lime

PINEAPPLE SALSA

150g peeled and cored pineapple, diced
1 fresh jalapeño chilli, finely diced
Finely grated zest and juice of 1 lime
3 tbsp coriander leaves, finely chopped

AVOCADO CREMA

2 small ripe avocados
100ml soured cream
1 tsp chipotle in adobo

TO SERVE

8 medium tortillas
150g red cabbage, finely shredded
Lime halves

1 Lay the tuna in a shallow tray and sprinkle with the chilli flakes, oregano, lime zest and salt on both sides. Trickle with the olive oil and turn the fish to coat well all over. Set aside in a cool place to marinate for an hour or so.

2 Meanwhile, to prepare the radishes, put them into a small bowl, sprinkle with a little salt and squeeze over the lime juice. Mix well and leave to pickle for an hour.

3 For the pineapple salsa, mix all the ingredients together in a bowl and set aside.

4 For the avocado crema, halve, peel, de-stone and chop the avocados then place in a blender or food processor with the soured cream and chipotle. Blitz until smoothly combined. Transfer to a serving bowl.

5 When you're ready to cook, lay the tuna steaks directly on the barbecue and cook for 1 minute on each side. Remove to a tray and leave to rest for a couple of minutes.

6 Meanwhile, place the tortillas on the barbecue for around 10 seconds on each side until warm and lightly charred but still pliable. Slice the tuna steaks.

7 To assemble the tacos, spread a spoonful of avocado crema on each tortilla and scatter over some shredded red cabbage. Add a couple of tuna slices and top with a spoonful of pineapple salsa and some pickled radish slices. Serve with lime halves for squeezing over.

WHOLE FISH BARBECUED IN NEWSPAPER

serves **2**

Wrapping this fish in paper means it steams as it cooks, trapping in
all those amazing aromatics from the lemongrass, ginger, lime leaves,
lemon and coriander. Don't skip pre-soaking the parcel in water – it
helps create the steam, and also stops the whole thing setting on fire ...!

1 bream, sea bass or John Dory
(about 600g), descaled and gutted

1 lemongrass stalk, bashed and cut
in half

1 spring onion, halved

4 thick slices of fresh ginger

2 kaffir lime leaves

1 lemon, thinly sliced

1 tbsp vegetable oil

Salt and freshly ground black pepper

CORIANDER AND LIME BUTTER

100g butter, softened

2 tbsp chopped coriander leaves

2 kaffir lime leaves, finely chopped

TO SERVE

Lime wedges

1 To prepare the bream, make deep parallel slashes
through the skin on both sides of the fish, at about 3cm
intervals. Put the lemongrass, spring onion, ginger and
kaffir lime leaves into the fish cavity.

2 Tear off a piece of baking paper about 15cm longer
than the fish and lay it on your work surface. Place a few
lemon slices down the middle of the paper and lay the fish
on top. Season both sides of the fish with salt and pepper
and drizzle with the oil. Place the remaining lemon slices
on top.

3 Wrap up the fish securely in the baking paper and
tie the ends tightly with kitchen string. A well-sealed
package will help the fish steam better. Now wrap the fish
in 2 or 3 layers of newspaper and tie again with string.

4 Shortly before cooking, immerse the whole package
in a bowl of cold water for 4–5 minutes, no longer.
Now place the fish parcel on the hottest part of your
barbecue and cook for 15–20 minutes, turning it over
after 8–10 minutes. The newspaper will burn but the
fish will steam to perfection inside.

5 While the fish is cooking, put the ingredients for the
coriander and lime butter into a small bowl and mix
until evenly combined. Season with salt and pepper.

6 Once the fish is cooked, remove the parcel from the
barbecue and open it up. Spread the butter over the fish
and let it melt. Serve with lime wedges for squeezing over.

TANDOORI FISH SKEWERS

Salmon has a high fat content so it stays lovely and moist when cooked over direct heat. It can also be eaten a bit pink in the middle, so you don't need to worry about undercooking it either. Quick pickled red onions cut through the rich flavours, as well as adding amazing colour.

. . . .

8 skinless salmon fillets (about 125g each)

2 large garlic cloves, grated

2.5cm piece of fresh ginger, grated

Juice of 1 lime

200g Greek yoghurt

1 tsp Kashmiri chilli powder

1 tsp ground turmeric

1 tsp ground cumin

2 tsp ground coriander

2 tsp sweet smoked paprika

A little vegetable oil to brush

Salt and freshly ground black pepper

PICKLED RED ONIONS

2 small red onions

125ml water

125ml white wine vinegar

½ tsp fennel seeds

½ tsp cumin seeds

1 tbsp salt

2 tbsp sugar

TO SERVE

Naan bread or roti

A handful of coriander leaves

1 long green chilli, finely sliced

Lime halves

Sweet chilli sauce

1 Prepare your pickled red onions an hour or so ahead. Slice the onions and place in a clean jar or bowl. Put the water, wine vinegar, fennel and cumin seeds, salt and sugar into a small pan over a medium heat and stir until the sugar and salt are fully dissolved. Pour the hot pickling liquor over the onions and leave to cool slightly. Pop the lid on (or cover the bowl) and place in the fridge to pickle.

2 To prepare the salmon, cut each fillet into 4 equal-sized chunks. Place these in a bowl with the garlic, ginger and lime juice and mix well.

3 In another bowl, mix the yoghurt with the spices and some salt and pepper. Add this spiced yoghurt to the salmon and mix well again. Leave to marinate in a cool place for at least 20 minutes, or up to an hour. Meanwhile, if using wooden skewers soak eight of them in water to avoid scorching on the barbecue.

4 Once marinated, thread the salmon onto your skewers, putting 4 chunks onto each skewer.

5 Brush the hot barbecue grid lightly with a little oil then lay the skewers on it. Cook for 2–3 minutes on each side until golden brown and lightly charred. Meanwhile, warm the naan or roti on the edge of the barbecue. Once cooked, transfer the skewers to a warm plate.

6 Serve the skewers on the warm naan or roti. Scatter over a little pickled red onion, some coriander and sliced green chilli. Serve with lime halves for squeezing over, and sweet chilli sauce on the side.

MACKEREL *with* MIXED PEPPER COUSCOUS

MACKEREL *with* MIXED PEPPER COUSCOUS

Readily available and inexpensive, mackerel is one of my favourite fish for barbecuing. The skin crisps up slightly on the grill and it has an amazing distinctive flavour. Infused oils, like this coriander, garlic and lime one, are an easy way of instantly boosting a dish.

8 medium mackerel fillets, pin-boned

12 rosemary sprigs

A good pinch of flaky salt

CORIANDER AND LEMON INFUSED OIL

100ml cold-pressed rapeseed oil

1 tbsp coriander seeds

3 garlic cloves, grated

Finely grated zest of 1 lemon

MIXED PEPPER COUSCOUS

350g couscous

350ml hot chicken (or vegetable) stock

3 peppers (ideally a mix of colours)

2 red chillies, deseeded and finely chopped

Finely grated zest and juice of 1 lime

3 plum tomatoes, finely chopped

A handful of flat-leaf parsley, finely chopped (including the stalks)

TO SERVE

Lemon wedges

Crusty bread

Green salad

1 First, put the couscous into a heatproof bowl. Bring the stock to the boil in a pan, pour onto the couscous and cover the bowl with cling film. Leave the couscous to cook in the residual heat and absorb the stock.

2 For the infused oil, pour the rapeseed oil into a small cast-iron pan and add the coriander seeds, garlic and lemon zest. Place the pan on the edge of the barbecue to gently warm the oil through for a few minutes. Remove from the heat and set aside to allow the flavours to infuse.

3 Cut the 'cheeks' from each pepper and lay them skin side down on the hot barbecue for 5–6 minutes or until the skin is blackened and blistered. Remove the charred peppers to a bowl, cover tightly with cling film and leave to steam for 5 minutes or so.

4 Now prepare the mackerel for cooking. Lay half of the rosemary sprigs on one side of your fish cage (you'll need a large one) and place the mackerel fillets side by side on the herb bed. Brush each mackerel fillet all over with the infused coriander and lemon oil and sprinkle with a little salt. Lay the remaining rosemary sprigs on top of the mackerel and close the fish cage. Set aside while you peel the roasted peppers.

5 Uncover the peppers and peel away their skins. Finely chop the pepper cheeks and place in a bowl. Add the chopped chillies, lime zest and juice, chopped tomatoes and parsley. Trickle over the remaining coriander and lemon infused oil and stir together while the peppers are warm, so that they soak up the flavours really well.

6 Place the fish cage on the hot barbecue and cook the fish for about 5 minutes on each side, turning the cage over once.

7 Uncover the couscous and fluff up gently with a fork. Add to the bowl of peppers and fork through. Season with salt and pepper to taste.

8 Transfer the pepper couscous to a warmed shallow serving dish. Remove the barbecued mackerel from the fish cage and arrange on top of the couscous. Serve at once, with lemon wedges, crusty bread and a green salad on the side.

Veggie

TENDER
CRUNCHY
MELTING

VEGGIE

Flame-grilling has the power to transform veg — even just a couple of minutes over some hot flames will elevate it into something really special. And you can barbecue almost any kind of vegetable. When it comes to introducing flavour, it's an incredibly versatile style of cooking. So, why not get a bit experimental and try out something new?

Veg can either be a centrepiece of your barbecue — as in my sweet potato and black bean burgers or courgette and halloumi skewers on pages 137 and 138 — or it can be part of a bigger menu. If you're putting together a barbecue feast, then the veg dishes and sides are so important to the overall balance of the meal.

The beauty of lots of the dishes in this chapter is that many of the elements can be made in advance and then those key grilled ingredients added just before serving, such as the

Mexican fiesta platter on page 151. This approach is particularly welcome if you don't want to spend ages manning the barbecue.

Think about using robust veg that won't fall apart or go mushy — chunky pieces of courgette, cabbage wedges, cauliflower florets, whole aubergines or a few new potatoes chucked onto the coals. Asparagus and purple sprouting broccoli are great on the barbecue too — just brush them with a bit of oil and cook them straight on the metal rack. You can barbecue most things, so just give it a go and see what happens. It's all trial and error, but nine times out of ten it'll be delicious. Barbecuing veg also gives you the opportunity to cook with the seasons — start off with some early spring asparagus and finish the year with winter squash.

As well as cooking veg on the grill, putting it directly on the coals can bring a whole new intensity of flavour

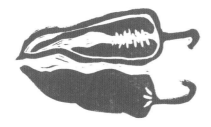

that is extra smoky and delicious. Consider the structure of the veg and this will help guide you in how to cook it: a potato is nice and firm so will survive being cooked on the coals, whereas a courgette or some mushrooms are more fragile and are best cooked up on the rack.

A good tip is to keep veggies whole where you can (whole peppers and tomatoes, for example) otherwise they can collapse and lose their juices. And it's completely fine if the outside goes blackened. This actually shows it's full of flavour. Just peel off the outer layer and all that amazing smokiness will have got right into the veg; you'll see I do this in the mixed pepper salad on page 134.

Grilling veg helps bring out all their natural sweetness, as the natural sugars in them caramelise – red onions are a brilliant example: they are already quite sweet but roasting them on the barbecue takes them to the next level. Flames and smoke give vegetables a whole new life and they can hold their own taste-wise against meatier counterparts, at the same time providing some much-needed crunch or a bit of freshness.

If you're putting on a veggie feast then cheese is a great way to give it some extra oomph too. Everyone loves a bit of melty cheese, and there are some great recipes that include cheese coming up. If you are going to barbecue cheese, go for Greek-style firm cheeses, like feta and halloumi – or 'squeaky cheese' as my son Acey likes to call it! These will hold their shape when they cook, unlike softer French-style cheeses or a classic Cheddar, which will melt completely.

With all those marinades and pops of flavour, you'll find veg will quickly become the star of your barbecue!

CHARRED AUBERGINE *with* MOZZARELLA AND TOMATO

serves 4

This is a restaurant-style dish with all the taste of the outdoors: wedges of grilled aubergine are drizzled in a warm garlic and rosemary olive oil dressing and served with creamy mozzarella, tomatoes and fresh basil – then finished with a little balsamic glaze.

2 large aubergines
2 tbsp extra virgin olive oil
5 ripe plum tomatoes, cut into wedges
2 x 200g balls of buffalo mozzarella
Salt and freshly ground black pepper

DRESSING

60ml extra virgin olive oil
1 large garlic clove, finely chopped
2 rosemary sprigs, finely chopped
40ml red wine vinegar

TO FINISH

2 tbsp balsamic glaze
A handful of basil leaves

1 Halve each aubergine lengthways and cut each half into 4 long wedges. Lay, cut side up, on a board and sprinkle with 1 tsp salt. Leave for 10 minutes, pat dry and flip them over. Repeat the process with the other side, then place on a tray.

2 When ready to cook, trickle the aubergines with the 2 tbsp olive oil and mix well with your hands so that both sides are well coated. Place on a medium-hot barbecue and cook for 3–4 minutes on each side – you want them to blacken a little in parts.

3 Meanwhile, to make the dressing, put the olive oil into a small cast-iron pan on the barbecue to heat up. Add the garlic and rosemary, stir and allow to sizzle for a minute or so. Remove the pan from the heat and immediately add the wine vinegar, to stop the cooking. Season with salt and pepper to taste.

4 Place the cooked aubergines in a deep-sided tray and pour on the dressing while they are still warm, to soak up all the flavours. Leave for at least 10 minutes, turning them over once.

5 When you are ready to serve, divide the aubergines and tomatoes between 4 serving plates and season with salt and pepper. Cut each mozzarella ball in half and add one half to each plate. Drizzle each plate with a little balsamic glaze and scatter over the basil leaves to serve.

BARBECUED MIXED PEPPER SALAD

This is a bright and colourful pepper salad with barbecued red onions, green olives, garlicky toasted sourdough and a great balsamic and sherry vinegar dressing. Charring the peppers makes it easier to peel off the skins and allows the smoky flavours to work right into the veg.

● ●

6 mixed peppers (red, green and yellow or orange)

2 red onions

200g sourdough, cut into 2.5cm thick slices

2 tbsp extra virgin olive oil, to drizzle

1 large garlic clove, halved

A large handful of flat parsley leaves

100g green olives, halved

Salt and freshly ground black pepper

DRESSING

60ml extra virgin olive oil

30ml sherry vinegar

1 tbsp balsamic vinegar

1 tsp Dijon mustard

1 Lay the peppers on a hot barbecue and turn regularly until they are lightly charred all over; this should take around 8 – 10 minutes. Remove from the barbecue, transfer to a bowl and cover tightly with cling film. Leave for around 15 minutes – the steam will help to loosen the skins.

2 Meanwhile, cut the red onions into quarters, keeping the root end intact (to hold them together during cooking). Place on the barbecue and cook for 8 – 10 minutes, turning occasionally, until lightly charred on all sides.

3 Drizzle both sides of the sourdough slices with olive oil and sprinkle with a little salt. Place on the barbecue and cook on both sides until well toasted. Remove the onions and bread from the barbecue and place on a tray to cool slightly. Rub each piece of toast with the cut surface of the garlic on both sides.

4 Uncover the peppers and peel away their skins. Remove the seeds and cut the pepper flesh into 2cm wide strips. Combine the peppers and onions in a large shallow serving dish. Tear the bread into bite-sized pieces and add to the salad with the parsley and green olives.

5 For the dressing, in a small bowl, whisk together the olive oil, sherry and balsamic vinegars and the mustard. Season with salt and pepper to taste.

6 Pour the dressing over the pepper salad and toss well. Leave for a few minutes so the bread can soak up the dressing then mix again. Let everyone help themselves.

SWEET POTATO and BLACK BEAN BURGERS

serves 6

It's all about the spicing in these veggie burgers – smoked paprika, cumin, garlic and chilli. Cooking the sweet potatoes directly in the coals makes them soft, squishy and even sweeter. Chopped nuts and breadcrumbs hold the burger mix together and provide a bit of bite.

2 large sweet potatoes (600g in total)

2 x 400g tins black beans, kidney beans or borlotti beans, drained and rinsed

75g panko breadcrumbs

80g roasted cashew nuts, finely chopped

1 tbsp ground cumin

2 tsp hot smoked paprika

1 tsp garlic powder

½ tsp chilli powder

1 tbsp vegetable oil

Salt and freshly ground black pepper

CHIPOTLE LIME MAYO

140g mayonnaise (or vegan mayo)

30g chipotle chillies in adobo sauce, finely chopped

Juice of ½ lime

TO ASSEMBLE AND SERVE

6 burger buns, split

6 slices of Cheddar or Gruyère (optional)

3 ripe avocados

Pickled jalapeño chillies (optional)

Lettuce or spinach leaves

1 Wait for the hot embers on your barbecue to turn white. Prick the sweet potatoes with a fork and wrap each one in foil. Tuck them into the coals and cook for about 40 minutes, turning every 10 minutes or so. Meanwhile, tip the beans into a large bowl and mash roughly with a fork.

2 Once cooked, unwrap the potatoes, let cool slightly then halve and scoop out the flesh directly onto the mashed beans. Add the breadcrumbs, cashews, spices and some salt and pepper. Mix well and check the seasoning. Divide into 6 portions and flatten into patties. Lay them on a tray, cover and place in the fridge to firm up for 1 hour.

3 After about 45 minutes, heat up your barbecue again. Mix the chipotle lime mayo ingredients together in a bowl until evenly combined; set aside.

4 Heat the 1 tbsp oil in a large cast-iron frying pan on the barbecue. Add the patties and cook for 3–4 minutes on each side. Once you've turned them, toast the burger bun halves on the barbecue; set aside on a tray. If using cheese, lay the slices on top of the patties, add a little water to the pan and cover with a lid – the steam created will help to melt the cheese. Halve, peel and de-stone the avocados, then slice lengthways, keeping them attached at the top.

5 To assemble the burgers, spread a spoonful of the mayo on the bottom half of each toasted bun. Add a pattie and lay a fanned avocado half on top. Spread more mayo on the bun top and sandwich the burger together, adding a few jalapeños if you'd like it extra spicy! Serve the salad leaves on the side.

COURGETTE and HALLOUMI SKEWERS

I love cooking halloumi on the barbecue. It caramelises beautifully on the outside but doesn't melt – perfect for kebabs! The salty flavour and firm texture work so well with grilled courgettes, which are a barbecue staple for me. A chilli and mint dressing gives the skewers a fresh lift.

• •

3 x 225g packs halloumi

3 medium courgettes (500g in total)

2 tbsp extra virgin olive oil

Salt and freshly ground black pepper

CHILLI MINT DRESSING

3 tbsp extra virgin olive oil

1 tbsp sherry vinegar

1 tbsp red wine vinegar

1 long red chilli, deseeded and finely diced

2 tbsp finely chopped mint leaves

1 tsp dried mint

1 You will need 16 short wooden skewers, 12cm long. Pre-soak them in water for 30 minutes to avoid scorching on the barbecue.

2 Cut the halloumi into 1cm batons. Do the same thing with the courgettes. Skewer a piece of halloumi onto each pair of skewers, placed parallel to each other 3–4cm apart, then thread a courgette baton on. Repeat until you have at least 3 pieces of halloumi and 3 courgette batons on each pair of skewers.

3 For the chilli mint dressing, put all the ingredients into a bowl, mix well to combine and season with salt and pepper to taste; set aside.

4 Brush both sides of each skewer with the olive oil and sprinkle with salt and pepper. Place on a medium heat on the barbecue and cook for around 3–4 minutes on each side. Once the halloumi is a lovely golden-brown colour, they are ready to remove from the heat.

5 Pile the courgette and halloumi skewers onto a warmed serving plate and spoon over the dressing. These are best served with a green salad on the side.

TOFU BURGERS *with* BEET AND RADISH PICKLE

With so much going on in every mouthful, these tofu burgers – with home-made pickle and citrusy yuzu mayo – will be a total winner if you're going meat-free. Tofu allows you to go really big on spice, so don't hold back!

• •

450g smoked tofu

Salt and freshly ground black pepper

MARINADE

2 tbsp barbecue sauce

50ml soy sauce (Kikkoman)

1 tbsp sesame oil

1 tbsp Sriracha hot sauce

1 tsp garlic powder

1 tsp onion powder

BEET AND RADISH PICKLE

200g raw beetroot, peeled

250ml rice vinegar

6 tbsp caster sugar

2 tsp coriander seeds

A bunch of radishes, thickly sliced

SPICED YUZU MAYO

120g mayonnaise

2 tsp yuzu juice

1 tbsp Sriracha hot sauce

TO ASSEMBLE

4 wholemeal burger buns, split

2 large tomatoes, thickly sliced (250g in total)

A handful of salad cress or alfalfa sprouts

160g carrot, grated

4 or 8 large lettuce leaves

1 Mix the marinade ingredients together in a shallow dish. Cut the smoked tofu into 4 equal-sized 'steaks' and add these to the marinade, turning to coat both sides. Leave to marinate for 20 minutes, or longer if you have the time.

2 Meanwhile, make the pickle. Thinly slice the beetroot and put into a small heatproof bowl. Combine the rice vinegar, sugar, coriander seeds and 2 tsp salt in a small pan and bring to the boil over a medium heat; stir to make sure the sugar and salt is fully dissolved. Strain this pickling liquor through a sieve onto the beetroot and leave to cool.

3 Once cooled, stir the radishes through the beetroot and leave to pickle for another 20 minutes, or longer if you can (the longer the better).

4 For the spiced yuzu mayo, mix the ingredients together in a small bowl until evenly combined and season with salt and pepper to taste.

5 When you are ready to cook, lift the tofu slices from the marinade and place them on the hot barbecue. Cook for 3–4 minutes on each side, basting with the marinade from time to time. Towards the end of cooking, toast the burger buns on the barbecue.

6 To assemble the burgers, spread a little mayo on each burger bun base. Add a few tomato slices, then some cress or alfalfa and grated carrot. Place a tofu steak on top. Finish with some pickle (well drained) and a big lettuce leaf or two. Spread more mayo on the burger bun lids, sandwich together and tuck in!

BARBECUED FETA TWO WAYS *and* FLATBREADS

serves **4 – 6**

Cooking feta in foil containers is an easy way to maximise flavour.
The feta warms through, coated in all the topping ingredients, and it's
an opportunity to get a bit experimental. Plus, there's almost no mess!
My yoghurt flatbreads are easy and puff up amazingly on the barbecue.

· ·

6 tbsp extra virgin olive oil
2 x 200g blocks of feta
Salt and freshly ground black pepper

SEEDED HONEY TOPPING

2 tbsp honey
2 tbsp sesame seeds, toasted
½ tsp nigella seeds
1 oregano sprig, leaves picked

TOMATO AND OLIVE TOPPING

80g cherry tomatoes, sliced
30g pitted Kalamata olives, sliced
1 oregano sprig, leaves picked

YOGHURT FLATBREADS

280g self-raising flour, plus extra to dust
250g natural yoghurt
2 tbsp extra virgin olive oil
1 tsp nigella seeds

TO SERVE

About 120g rocket leaves

1 First prepare the flatbreads. In a large bowl, mix the flour, yoghurt and olive oil together with a large pinch of salt and a grinding of pepper, to form a smooth dough. Tip onto a floured surface and knead well for a few minutes. Place in a bowl and leave to rest for 30 minutes.

2 Once rested, divide the dough into 6 even-sized balls. Dust the surface of each ball with a little more flour and roll out thinly. Sprinkle with the nigella seeds and roll each flatbread one more time to embed the seeds into the dough. Sprinkle with flour and lay the flatbreads one top of the other – ready to barbecue.

3 For the barbecued feta, you will need two fairly deep foil trays, each large enough to hold a block of feta snugly (or you could create two containers from doubled sheets of foil).

4 For the seeded honey feta, pour 1½ tbsp olive oil into the centre of one foil tray and lay one of the feta blocks on top. Trickle the honey over the feta and sprinkle with the sesame and nigella seeds and the oregano leaves. Season lightly and drizzle over another 1½ tbsp olive oil. Put the lid on (or wrap up the foil tightly to seal).

5 For the tomato and olive feta, pour 1½ tbsp olive oil into the centre of the other foil tray and lay the second feta block on top. Arrange the sliced tomatoes on the feta and scatter over the olives and oregano leaves. Drizzle with the rest of the oil and season with salt and pepper. Put the lid on the container (or wrap up the foil tightly to seal).

6 Place the foil trays (or parcels) on a hot barbecue for 10 minutes. Towards the end of cooking, lay a few flatbreads on the barbecue around the feta containers and cook for 1–2 minutes. If the flatbreads puff up a little, pierce the bubbles with your tongs. Flip them over gently and cook for another 2 minutes or until well browned.

7 Lift the feta containers off the barbecue and remove the lids (or open up the foil). Place back on the barbecue and put the barbecue lid on to finish cooking the feta for a few minutes.

8 Remove the feta from the barbecue and place on a serving platter with a bowl of rocket and the flatbreads, cut into wedges. Let everyone help themselves.

CAULIFLOWER STEAKS *with* FREEKEH SALAD

serves 4

Freekeh is a fantastic grain that takes on other flavours well, and adds great texture to this Middle Eastern salad. It's like next level couscous! The salad is topped with chunky cauliflower steaks that are coated in an aromatic spice mix, and enhanced by the smoke from the barbecue.

2 large cauliflowers

2 tsp ras el hanout

½ tsp ground turmeric

½ tsp sweet smoked paprika

4 tbsp olive oil

Salt and freshly ground black pepper

FREEKEH SALAD

2 x 250g pouches ready-to-eat freekeh

300g cucumber, diced

1 red onion, diced

2 large handfuls of mint leaves, roughly chopped

2 large handfuls of flat-leaf parsley, roughly chopped

DRESSING

120g Greek yoghurt

2 tbsp tahini

Juice of ½ lemon

2 tbsp extra virgin olive oil

TO SERVE

4 tbsp pomegranate molasses

40g pistachio nuts, roughly chopped

50g pomegranate seeds

1 Cut right through the middle of each cauliflower and then cut a large 4cm thick steak from each half. (Keep the offcuts to use in a salad or make cauliflower rice for another dish.)

2 In a small bowl, mix the ras el hanout, turmeric, smoked paprika, 2 big pinches of salt and a grinding of pepper with the olive oil. Brush the spicy oil all over the cauliflower steaks to coat both sides evenly.

3 For the salad, put the freekeh, cucumber, red onion and chopped herbs into a large bowl and mix well.

4 For the dressing, in a separate bowl, combine the yoghurt, tahini, lemon juice and olive oil. Season well with salt and pepper and whisk until smooth. If it is a little too thick, stir in 1–2 tbsp water to loosen. Pour the dressing over the freekeh and stir well; set aside.

5 Place the cauliflower steaks on a medium-hot part of the barbecue and cook for 4–5 minutes on each side or until tender and charred lightly in places.

6 Spoon the freekeh onto serving plates and top each portion with a cooked cauliflower steak. Drizzle a little pomegranate molasses over the top and sprinkle with chopped pistachios and pomegranate seeds to serve.

STUFFED SWEET POTATOES

serves **4**

Take baked spuds to new heights with these coal-cooked sweet potatoes filled with soured cream, chives, bacon and melted cheese. They become soft and even sweeter as they cook in their foil parcels, absorbing all that lovely smokiness.

4 medium sweet potatoes

2 tbsp extra virgin olive oil

Salt and freshly ground black pepper

TOPPINGS

1 tsp sweet smoked paprika

120g Cheddar, freshly grated

6 slices of thick-cut smoked streaky bacon (optional)

4 heaped tbsp soured cream

8–10 chives, cut into 1cm lengths

1 Tear 4 pieces of foil, each large enough to wrap a sweet potato. Using a fork, pierce each sweet potato all over then place one in the middle of each piece of foil. Drizzle with the olive oil and sprinkle with salt and pepper. Rub the sweet potatoes well so they are evenly coated, then wrap in the foil.

2 Place the foil-wrapped potatoes on the grid of a hot barbecue and cook, turning them regularly; they will take around 45–50 minutes depending on their size. You can tell when they are cooked by pressing them down with your tongs – if they feel softened, they are ready. Remove them from the barbecue and open up the foil.

3 Make a cut along the middle of each sweet potato and push the two sides slightly apart. Sprinkle the exposed potato flesh with the smoked paprika and grated cheese. Keep the sweet potatoes in their foil and pop them back on the barbecue, then close the lid for a few minutes to melt the cheese.

4 Meanwhile, if you're happy with a non-veggie version, barbecue the bacon until browned and crispy on both sides; remove and chop roughly. If the cheese still hasn't melted, pop the lid on the barbecue for a few minutes.

5 Remove the potatoes from the barbecue and place on a serving tray. Spoon on the soured cream, add the bacon pieces if using and sprinkle with the snipped chives. Serve straight away.

MEXICAN FIESTA PLATTER

serves **4 – 6**

Flame-grilled corn-on-the-cob is out of this world. Mixed with kidney beans, coriander, chilli and lime and served with a cooling avocado cream and crunchy corn chips, this is a veggie feast – Mexican-style. Keep a close eye on the corn, as it can burn quickly on the barbecue.

● ●

4 corn-on-the-cob

1 tsp smoked paprika

5 tbsp extra virgin olive oil

10 spring onions

400g tin kidney beans, rinsed and drained

Juice of ½ lime

A large handful of coriander, roughly chopped

1 long red chilli, thinly sliced

Sea salt and freshly ground black pepper

AVOCADO CREAM

3 large ripe avocados

Juice of ½ lime

10 dashes of Tabasco

5 tbsp soured cream

TO SERVE

Corn chips

1 Lay the corn cobs in a large deep roasting tray and pour on 300ml water. Cover with foil, place on a hot barbecue and put the lid on. Allow to steam for 15 minutes then remove the corn cobs from the barbecue, transfer them to a shallow tray and let cool slightly.

2 Sprinkle the corn with the smoked paprika and 1 tsp sea salt. Drizzle with 2 tbsp olive oil and turn the corn cobs to coat. Add the spring onions to the tray, drizzle with 1 tbsp oil and sprinkle with a little salt; toss to coat.

3 For the avocado cream, halve and de-stone the avocados, then scoop out the flesh into a blender or food processor. Add the lime juice, Tabasco, soured cream and some salt and pepper. Blitz until smoothly combined.

4 Place the corn cobs on the barbecue over a medium heat – near the hot coals but not directly over them. Cook, turning every few minutes, for about 15 minutes until lightly charred all over. Remove the corn to a plate and leave to cool slightly. Add the spring onions to the barbecue and cook for 2–3 minutes on each side.

5 Stand the corn cobs upright on a board and run a sharp knife down each side, to shave off the kernels. Cut the spring onions into 2cm lengths. Combine in a large bowl. Add the kidney beans, lime juice, chopped coriander and remaining 2 tbsp olive oil. Mix well and season to taste.

6 Spread the avocado cream in your serving dish. Pile the corn mixture on top and scatter over the red chilli. Serve with a big bowl of corn chips for dipping.

UMAMI MUSHROOM *and* HALLOUMI BURGERS

serves 4

These super-juicy mushroom burgers are packed full of big umami flavours. The dried porcini powder in the butter adds an incredible savoury depth, which is enhanced with chilli, garlic and lemon zest. A thick slice of glazed halloumi makes each burger satisfyingly chunky.

2 x 225g packs halloumi

8 portobello mushrooms, stems removed

UMAMI BUTTER

160g butter, softened

2 tbsp white miso

1 tbsp light soy sauce

5g dried porcini mushrooms, ground to a powder

½ tsp dried chilli flakes

2 large garlic cloves, finely grated

Finely grated zest of ½ lemon

Salt and freshly ground black pepper

TO ASSEMBLE

4 brioche burger buns, split

4 tbsp sweet chilli or hot chilli sauce

4 tbsp mayonnaise

About 60g rocket leaves

1 Cut each block of halloumi in half horizontally through the middle to create 4 flat halloumi steaks in total.

2 For the umami butter, put all the ingredients into a bowl and mix until evenly combined, seasoning with a good pinch each of salt and pepper.

3 Brush the portobello mushrooms on one side with the umami butter and place them buttered side down on a medium-hot barbecue. Brush the other side thickly with butter while they are cooking. Turn the mushrooms over after 2–3 minutes and add the halloumi to the barbecue. Brush the surface of the halloumi with umami butter too. Keep brushing the mushrooms with the butter as they cook; do the same with the halloumi.

4 Towards the end of the cooking, toast the burger buns on the barbecue. Brush any remaining umami butter onto the toasted buns.

5 To assemble the burgers, place a mushroom, flat side up, on the base of each burger bun. Top with a halloumi steak and add a spoonful of sweet chilli or hot chilli sauce. Pile a big handful of rocket leaves on top. Spread some mayo on the bun lids and sandwich the burgers together. Tuck in straight away.

TIP

Use a coffee grinder to grind any extra dried mushrooms. Keep the mushroom powder in a sealed jar and use it to add flavour to pasta sauces, soups, stews etc.

Open Fire

FLAMES

INSTINCT

OUTDOORS

OPEN FIRE

· ·

When it's just you and the flames, it takes everything right back to basics. Cooking over an open fire is instinctive and it can be a bit unpredictable, but that just makes it even more exciting! Many of us have memories of cooking on a campfire as kids – it feels like such an adventure. But it's not just about baked potatoes and beans. You can cook most things on an open fire in the same way you would on a barbecue – you just need to set a metal rack over the top.

You can also use an open fire like a hob and put a frying pan or saucepan either on the rack or straight in the embers, so you can create some great one-pot meals. All that fire and smoke will boost the flavour in your food.

Open-fire cooking can be a bit harder to control than a barbecue, especially if your barbecue is one with a lid and air vents that you can open and close to help adjust the heat. But the principles are the same, you just need to be a little more aware of what your food is doing and keep checking it to make sure it doesn't burn. It's all part of the experience!

The recipes in this chapter are really flexible and a lot of fun to make – perfect for your next camping trip and for getting the kids to help. Start the day off right with the breakfast muffins or kimchi toasties (on pages 158 and 160). And after a long day in the fresh air my chipotle bean chilli on page 167 will get everyone warmed up.

Or if you want to try something a bit special, try the grilled lemon sole on page 171. Cooking over fire creates a fantastic atmosphere. I have a great memory from a trip to Argentina of cooking thick salted pork chops on an asador (which is like an open fire pit) out in the fields. It was so simple, but tasted unbelievable and it was such an amazing experience being out under the open skies.

There are a few things to bear in mind when you're cooking on a fire: if you're using a fire pit, the kind people have in their gardens, just be aware that it can get quite messy from the cooking juices dripping down into it, so you'll have to give it a good clean afterwards. If it's a particularly fancy fire pit, then it might be better to stick to the dishes cooked in a pan.

It goes without saying that you should check you're permitted to light a fire wherever you happen to be. Make quite sure it's safe to light one, and keep control over it — never leave an open fire unattended.

Open-fire cooking brings people together like nothing else — sitting round toasting marshmallows or cooking sausages on skewers is a great way to spend some quality time with friends and family. So whether you're cooking on a campfire under the stars or on a fire pit in your back garden, let these recipes bring out your inner caveman or woman!

BREAKFAST MUFFINS

serves **4**

When you've woken up in your tent (perhaps after a bad night's sleep!) these are just the thing to put a smile back on your face. Prep them in advance so they're ready to go in the morning. Sausage, bacon, egg and cheese – it's a fry-up in a bun and the best way to start the day.

• •

4 Cumberland pork sausages

1 tbsp light olive oil

4 rashers of smoked streaky bacon, cut in half

4 slices of Cheddar

4 free-range eggs

Salt and freshly ground black pepper

TO ASSEMBLE

4 English muffins, split

50g butter, softened

Tomato ketchup, chilli sauce, HP sauce or barbecue sauce

4 tbsp crispy onions (shop-bought)

1 Slit the skin along one side of each sausage and peel it away. Place the sausage meat in an egg ring or crumpet ring and flatten down to form a pattie. Repeat with the remaining 3 sausages.

2 Place a large cast-iron pan on a grid over your fire. When it is hot, add the oil. Now place the 4 sausage patties in the pan and flatten each one down with the back of a fish slice. Cook for 2 minutes on one side.

3 Flip the patties over and add the bacon to the pan. Cook for 2 minutes, turning the bacon after a minute or so – you want it brown and crispy. Lay a slice of cheese on each of the sausage patties and leave to melt in the pan.

4 Meanwhile, toast the split muffins over the fire. At the same time, crack the eggs into the pan (into egg or crumpet rings if you like) and season with salt and pepper. Fry for a few minutes until cooked to your liking.

5 Spread the muffins with the butter. Place a muffin base on each plate and top with a sausage pattie and a shake of your favourite sauce. Place a fried egg on top and lay the bacon over the egg. Sprinkle liberally with crispy onions. Sandwich together with the muffin lid, grab napkins and enjoy!

KIMCHI *and* CHEESE TOASTIES

makes 2

Kimchi is king in these oozy and decadent pan-fried toasties. Its vinegary sharpness cuts through the richness of the melted cheese and adds a bit of crunch. Cook these toasties nice and slowly so they get properly gooey all the way through without the bread burning.

4 thick slices of sourdough

40g butter, softened

150g Cheddar or mozzarella (or a mix), grated

150g kimchi, drained and patted dry

2 spring onions, finely sliced

1 long green chilli, finely sliced

50g baby spinach

1 tbsp light olive oil

Salt and freshly ground black pepper

1 Butter the 4 slices of sourdough thickly on both sides with the softened butter. Lay 2 slices on a board and sprinkle each with a quarter of the cheese.

2 Add a layer of kimchi, then sprinkle with the spring onions and green chilli slices. Lay the spinach leaves over them and top with the remaining grated cheese. Season with a little salt and pepper and sandwich together with the other slices of bread.

3 Place a large non-stick cast-iron frying pan on a grid over your fire and when it is hot, add the olive oil. Place the 2 sandwiches in the pan and cook gently for around 5 minutes on each side. You want the bread to turn a lovely golden brown and for the cheese to melt completely on the inside, so go gently! It will take a little while but it will be so worth it in the end.

4 Remove the toasties from the pan and cut each one in half with a serrated knife. Enjoy them while they are hot but try not to burn your lips!

TIP

Make sure you pat the kimchi thoroughly dry with kitchen paper so it doesn't make your toasties soggy.

HALLOUMI BREAKFAST BUNS

serves **2**

Halloumi, eggs, spinach and avocado taste amazing together, but it's the tomato relish that really brings them alive in these veggie breakfast buns. Make the relish at home and take it with you in a jar – it's the little extras like this that will elevate your campfire cooking.

TOMATO RELISH

2 tbsp rapeseed oil

1 tsp mustard seeds

½ tsp cumin seeds

1 medium onion, finely chopped

¼ tsp dried chilli flakes

2 tbsp white wine vinegar

2 tbsp soft light brown sugar

400g tin chopped tomatoes

Salt and freshly ground black pepper

BREAKFAST BUNS

225g pack halloumi

1 tbsp light olive oil

2 wholemeal bread rolls, split

1 avocado

2 large free-range eggs

40g butter

2 handfuls of baby spinach

1 To make the tomato relish, place a small pan over a medium-high heat on the hob. When hot, add the oil then the mustard and cumin seeds. As they begin to sizzle, add the onion and cook, stirring regularly, for 4–5 minutes. Add the chilli flakes and cook for 1–2 minutes.

2 Stir in the wine vinegar and sugar and let bubble for a minute or so before adding the tomatoes with some seasoning. Bring back to the boil, lower the heat and simmer gently for about 15 minutes until reduced and thickened. Take off the heat, taste to check the seasoning and leave to cool. If you're making the relish well ahead, transfer it to a jar and pop it in the fridge.

3 When you're ready to cook, slice the halloumi block horizontally in half to create 2 flat steaks. Place a large cast-iron pan on a grid over your fire and add the olive oil. When hot, add the halloumi and cook for 2–3 minutes on each side, until golden and crispy. Meanwhile, toast the bread rolls over the fire.

4 Add the eggs to the pan and season them. Halve, peel, de-stone and slice the avocado; set aside. Once the halloumi steaks are cooked, remove from the pan and set aside on a warmed plate. Add half the butter to the pan, let it melt, then toss in the spinach. Season and let it just wilt.

5 Butter the toasted bread rolls. Spoon some tomato relish onto the base of each roll and top with a halloumi steak. Pile the spinach on top and add the fried egg and avocado slices. Sandwich with the tops of the rolls and tuck in.

CHICKEN LIVERS *and* WILD MUSHROOMS ON TOAST

serves 4

Caramelised chicken livers are piled onto warm focaccia with wild mushrooms, garlic and greens … lush. If you're planning to do it on a camping trip, soak the livers and prepare the coating before you go, and pack them to take with you. Serve a fried egg on top, if you like.

• •

300g chicken livers

About 150ml milk

SEASONED COATING

10g mushroom powder

50g plain flour

½ tsp dried rosemary

½ tsp garlic powder

1 tsp salt

TO ASSEMBLE AND COOK

1 small focaccia, cut into 4 big wedges

A splash of olive oil

50g butter

3 banana shallots, finely diced

2 garlic cloves, sliced

100g wild mushrooms, cleaned

100g wild garlic leaves or cavolo nero, finely shredded

25ml Marsala (optional)

TO FINISH

2 tsp balsamic vinegar

50g Parmesan, freshly grated or shaved

1 Prepare the chicken livers the evening before. Trim out any white membrane and sinew then place the livers in a small bowl and pour on enough milk to just cover. Cover and leave the chicken livers to soak in the fridge overnight – to draw out any bitterness.

2 The next day, drain the chicken livers, put them into a container and seal. For the coating, put the ingredients into another container, pop the lid on and give it a shake to mix well. Pack both containers for your campfire.

3 Wait until your fire calms down a little before you start cooking. Pat the chicken livers dry with kitchen paper. Add them to the seasoned flour and toss to coat all over.

4 Toast the focaccia over the fire or hot coals, using a pair of tongs, until the bread has a few charred edges. Set aside on a warm plate; keep warm.

5 Place a wide cast-iron pan directly on the embers to heat up then add a splash of olive oil with the butter. When the butter is melted and starting to foam, place the chicken livers in the pan. Fry for a minute or so to colour, then turn the livers over and throw in the shallots, garlic, mushrooms and shredded greens. Stir-fry for a minute or two until the leaves just wilt. Add the Marsala if using, stir and scrape to deglaze the pan then take off the heat.

6 Divide the liver and mushroom mix between the toasted focaccia and drizzle with a little balsamic vinegar. Sprinkle with Parmesan and serve at once.

CHIPOTLE MIXED BEAN CHILLI

serves **4 – 6**

There's a risk that vegan meals feel like they're missing a main 'focal point'. That's when a chilli like this really comes into its own! Filling and delicious, packed with punchy flavours, and served with avocado salsa and crunchy corn chips on the side, every part is unmissable.

1 large red pepper

1 large green pepper

2 tbsp light olive oil

2 onions, diced

2 large garlic cloves, finely chopped

1½ tsp ground cumin

1½ tsp sweet smoked paprika

1 tsp garlic powder

2 tbsp tomato purée

2 tbsp chipotle paste

1 vegetable stock cube

500ml water

400g tin chopped tomatoes

400g tin black beans

400g tin borlotti beans

400g tin mixed beans

Salt and freshly ground black pepper

AVOCADO SALSA

2 ripe avocados

A handful of coriander, chopped

Juice of ½ lime

TO SERVE

100g pickled sliced jalapeño chillies

200g corn chips

1 Place a Dutch oven or large cast-iron casserole on a grid over your fire to heat up. Meanwhile, halve, core and deseed the peppers then cut into 2.5cm pieces. When the casserole is hot, add the olive oil then toss in the onions. Fry, stirring, for 3–4 minutes until starting to soften. Add the garlic and cook for 1–2 minutes.

2 Add the diced peppers to the pan and stir well. Sprinkle in the ground cumin, smoked paprika and garlic powder and continue to cook, stirring, for 1–2 minutes to cook out the spices. Add the tomato purée and chipotle paste, stir well and cook for another minute.

3 Crumble in the stock cube, then pour in the water and tip the chopped tomatoes into the pan. Stir well and bring to the boil. Drain all the beans and add them to the pan. Stir well and simmer for 15–20 minutes until the liquor is reduced and thickened.

4 Meanwhile, to make your avocado salsa, halve, peel and de-stone the avocados, then chop the flesh. Tip into a bowl, add the chopped coriander and lime juice and stir to mix. Season with salt and pepper to taste and stir again.

5 Just before the chilli is ready, taste and give it a little seasoning if it needs it. Serve the chilli in warmed bowls, adding a big spoonful of avocado salsa to each bowl. Top with a few jalapeño slices and add a big handful of corn chips. Enjoy!

POTATO, PEA *and* HAM TORTILLA

serves **6 – 8**

This versatile one-pan dish is made with potatoes, eggs, ham, frozen peas and cheese – basics you can pick up pretty much anywhere, even if you're staying on a campsite. Manchego has a nutty flavour that goes well with the sweetness of the peas, but you can use any hard cheese.

• •

400g potatoes

50ml extra virgin olive oil

1 large onion, halved and thinly sliced

120g thickly sliced ham, cut into 2cm pieces

150g frozen peas

8 large free-range eggs

50g Manchego (or other hard cheese), grated

2 tbsp herb leaves (basil, thyme or parsley), finely chopped

Salt and freshly ground black pepper

1 Peel the potatoes and cut into 2cm cubes. Place in a saucepan and cover with water. Bring to the boil and cook for 10 minutes or until tender. Drain and set aside.

2 Place a 26cm non-stick cast-iron frying pan on a grid over your fire. When hot, add the olive oil then the onion and cook, stirring, for 3–4 minutes or until the onion is starting to brown slightly. Add the ham and cook for another 2 minutes, then toss in the potatoes and stir well. Add the peas and cook for another couple of minutes.

3 Meanwhile, crack the eggs into a bowl and season generously with salt and pepper. Add the grated cheese and chopped herbs and beat to combine.

4 Pour the egg mixture into pan and cook for 4–5 minutes. You should be able to run a rubber spatula around the edge and, if you shake the pan, the tortilla shouldn't be sticking. If the egg has set around the edges but is still a little runny in the middle, it's ready to flip! Take the pan off the fire and invert a large plate over it. Holding the pan and the plate together, flip them over to turn out the tortilla onto the plate.

5 Slide the tortilla back into the pan and place back over the fire. Tuck in the edges with the spatula and cook for another minute. This would keep it a touch gooey in the centre. Cook for an extra minute or two if you prefer.

6 Remove the tortilla from the pan and serve immediately. It can be eaten hot or cold. A big green salad and a bowl of slaw on the side would be perfect.

LEMON SOLE *with* SHRIMP AND BROWN BUTTER SAUCE

serves 2

Flat fish like lemon sole have a lovely subtle taste that absorbs the smokiness from outdoor cooking really well. Dusting the fish in flour produces a light crispy coating, but it's the shrimp and brown butter sauce that turns this into a really special fish supper.

50g plain flour

100ml vegetable oil

12 chunky asparagus spears

2 lemon soles or other small flat fish (about 450g each), white skin removed (ask your fishmonger to do this)

2 tbsp olive oil

A handful of lemon thyme sprigs

1 lemon, cut in half

Salt and freshly ground black pepper

SHRIMP AND BROWN BUTTER SAUCE

100g butter

¼ tsp ground mace

½ tsp freshly grated ginger

Juice of ½ lemon

70g brown shrimps

2 tsp roughly chopped dill

1 When you're ready to start, season the flour with 1 tsp salt and spread out on a small tray or flat plate. Pour the 100ml vegetable oil into another tray.

2 To prepare the asparagus, bend each spear near the base until it snaps and discard the woody ends. Lay the asparagus spears in a shallow tray.

3 Now prepare the sauce. In a small pan over a medium-high heat, melt the butter with the mace and ginger and cook until golden brown. Remove from the heat and add the lemon juice, shrimps and chopped dill; keep warm.

4 Lay the fish on the seasoned flour and turn it to coat both sides, then dip each fish into the vegetable oil and turn again to coat both sides, making sure there are no dry patches. Lay the fish, skin side down, on a grid over the fire on a medium heat. Leave it to cook and char for 5 minutes. Meanwhile, drizzle the asparagus with the olive oil and season with salt and pepper.

5 Once the skin is crispy, carefully flip the fish over using a large fish slice or palette knife and scatter the thyme sprigs over the top. Lay the asparagus spears directly on the grid at this point, along with the lemon halves, placing them flesh side down. Barbecue for 3–4 minutes until the fish is just cooked and the asparagus is tender, turning the spears to ensure they colour all over.

6 Lift the fish off the grill, along with the asparagus and lemon halves, onto warmed serving plates. Spoon on the shrimp and brown butter sauce and serve at once.

CEDAR PLANKED SALMON *with* HERBS AND LEMON

serves 4

This brilliant recipe needs to be cooked on a fire pit fuelled with logs or lumpwood charcoal. You also want a cedar barbecue board, a hammer and some long nails (to secure the salmon to the board), plus a brick to sit this on. The result is fantastic – almost like hot-smoking.

A bunch of thyme

A bunch of rosemary

1 lemon, cut into 8 slices

1 tsp rapeseed oil

½ side of salmon (about 750g), cut from the tail end

1 tsp flaky salt

½ tsp cracked black pepper

½ tsp caraway seeds

1 Pre-soak your cedar board in cold water for 30 minutes before you intend to use it, then place on a flat surface. Lay the thyme and half of the rosemary on the board and place the lemon slices on top. Lay the salmon on the bed.

2 Brush the salmon lightly with the oil and season with the salt, pepper and caraway. Cut 3 or 4 sprigs of rosemary into 2cm lengths and press into the salmon flesh. Secure the salmon to the board by hammering in a few nails.

3 Once the flames have started to die down a little in your fire pit, move all the coals to one side, to create a slightly cooler side. Place a brick in the fire pit, next to the hot coals. Now lay the cedar board on the brick with the thickest side of the fish closest to the hot embers. Cook for about 30 minutes, rotating the board every 5 minutes; this will cook the fish from the sides and underneath.

4 To give the middle of the fish a boost: scoop up a good amount of hot embers with a barbecue shovel, pile on top the fish and leave to finish cooking for 5 minutes (as pictured on page 15). This will slightly char the fish and give an incredible flavour.

5 Brush the hot coals off the fish and lift the salmon on its board out of the fire pit. To check it is cooked, lightly press the thickest part with your thumb to see if the flesh starts to flake. If it needs a little longer just cover with the coals again and cook for another 5 minutes.

6 Once the fish is cooked, set aside to rest for 5 minutes. Portion or flake the salmon and serve with a big salad.

MAPLE GLAZED BUTTERFLIED LEG OF LAMB

MAPLE GLAZED BUTTERFLIED LEG OF LAMB

serves **6 – 8**

This recipe is best cooked over a fire pit of beech wood. It's definitely one to make when you want to show off. In many ways it is a very simple recipe, but it does require a good feel for temperature and fire control and you need to stay with it — no wandering off!

1 boned leg of lamb (about 2.25kg), butterflied (ask your butcher to do this)

10 rosemary sprigs

3 tbsp olive oil

2 tbsp fennel seeds

2 red onions

Salt and freshly ground black pepper

MAPLE, MUSTARD AND MARMITE GLAZE

100ml maple syrup

50g Dijon mustard

50g Marmite

MINT DRESSING

80ml extra virgin olive oil

4 tbsp red wine vinegar

½ bunch of mint, leaves picked and roughly chopped

1 Lay the lamb out flat on a board, skin side up. Using a small sharp knife, make small slits in the skin all over the surface, and then turn and repeat on the flesh side. Break off small pieces of rosemary and poke these into the slits. Rub the olive oil all over the lamb and sprinkle with the fennel seeds.

2 Carefully press 2 robust long skewers through the middle of the flattened lamb at right angles to each other, so they form a cross. Skewer a whole red onion on the end of each skewer and press up against the lamb; these will act as a guard from the direct heat and hold the lamb in place (as pictured on the opposite page, left). Season the lamb all over with 2 tsp salt and lots of pepper.

3 When you're ready to start cooking, you first need to warm the lamb over the fire pit – thread the skewers through the bars of the pit so that the lamb is suspended at an angle, over the fire (as pictured on the opposite page, centre). Leave to warm gently for 25 minutes or so, then turn the lamb and repeat. Check the internal temperature with a meat thermometer: it should register 55–60°C; it will only take on a little colour at this stage.

4 Meanwhile, for the glaze, put the maple syrup into a small saucepan and bring to a simmer, then stir in the mustard and Marmite. Take off the heat and set aside.

5 For the dressing, simply mix all the ingredients together in a small bowl and season with salt and pepper to taste; keep to one side.

6 Once the meat is warmed to the desired temperature, lift the skewers and lay the lamb skin side down on the metal rack so the fat starts to roast and render. Once you get a good colour to the skin, turn the meat over and cook for 10 minutes.

7 Brush the lamb with the glaze and cook for a further 10 minutes, turning it halfway. If the meat seems to be colouring too quickly, lift it off and place two bricks on the grill (parallel and apart) then suspend the skewered lamb from them to move it away from the heat slightly (as pictured above, right).

8 Once cooked, transfer the lamb to a warmed platter, cover with foil and leave to rest for 10–15 minutes. When rested, sprinkle with a little flaky salt. Carve the lamb and lay on the platter, spoon the dressing over liberally and place on the table for everyone to help themselves.

SMOKY SPICED PULLED PORK HUEVOS

serves 4

I can just imagine a bunch of cowboys cooking this smoky pulled-pork stew, sitting round a big cast-iron pot. Eggs are baked into the stew, a bit of cheese is melted on top, then it's all scooped up with warm tortillas. The chilli-tomato base sauce has amazing Mexican flavours.

2 tbsp vegetable oil

2 onions, diced

4 garlic cloves, finely grated

2 tbsp tomato purée

2 tbsp red wine vinegar

1 tbsp agave syrup or muscovado sugar

400g pulled pork (leftover or shop-bought)

200ml water

4 tbsp Cholula hot sauce

1 tbsp ancho chilli flakes

500g mixed cherry tomatoes, halved

3 fresh jalapeño chillies, sliced

4 large eggs

50g Cheddar or Monterey Jack, grated

A handful of coriander, leaves picked

4 spring onions, sliced

Salt and cayenne pepper

TO SERVE

Soured cream

2 limes, cut into wedges

Tortillas or corn chips

1 Heat a large, wide cast-iron pan (one that has a lid) on your open fire. When it is hot, add the oil and then the onions. Cook over a high heat, stirring often, for about 10 minutes until softened and starting to caramelise.

2 Add the garlic and tomato purée, stir well and cook for a few minutes, then pour in the wine vinegar and stir in the agave or sugar. Let bubble to reduce to a glaze. Add the chopped pulled pork and turn to coat in the glaze.

3 Pour on the water to cover and add the hot sauce and chilli flakes. Bring to a simmer, stir well and toss in the tomatoes and jalapeños. Return to a simmer and cook until the tomatoes just begin to soften slightly. Season with salt and cayenne to taste.

4 Now crack the 4 eggs on top of the porky spiced salsa and sprinkle over the cheese. Put a lid on the pan, so that the eggs steam and cook for 8 minutes or so. Take the pan off the fire, remove the lid and scatter the coriander and spring onions over everything.

5 Spoon into warmed serving bowls and serve straight away, with soured cream, lime wedges and warm tortillas or corn chips for dipping.

SPICY SAUSAGE BAKED BEANS

After a day outdoors, this posh version of sausage and baked beans is rich and satisfying. The addition of chorizo brings that lovely paprika heat and sweet smokiness that complements campfire cooking so nicely. Make sure you have lots of flame-toasted bread to mop up the juices.

Vegetable oil for cooking

1 large onion, diced

1½ good-quality cooking chorizo rings (about 360g in total), thickly sliced

150g piece of streaky bacon, cut into lardons

3 garlic cloves, finely chopped

2 tsp smoked paprika

2 tsp tomato purée

50g caster sugar

100ml red wine vinegar

100ml red wine

2 x 400g tins chopped tomatoes

2 bay leaves

2 thyme sprigs

4 good-quality butcher's sausages

2 x 400g tins cannellini or other white beans, drained

4 thick slices of sourdough

80g butter, softened

1 Place a Dutch oven or large cast-iron casserole on a grid over your fire to heat up then add a splash of oil. Toss in the onion and fry, stirring, for 3–4 minutes until starting to soften. Add the chorizo slices to the pan and cook for 1–2 minutes. Toss in the lardons and cook in the lovely chorizo oil for a further 2–3 minutes.

2 Stir in the garlic and cook for a minute, then add the smoked paprika and tomato purée and cook, stirring, for a couple of minutes. Add the sugar then pour in the wine vinegar and red wine. Stir well and let the liquor reduce to a glaze.

3 Now add the tinned tomatoes, bay leaves and thyme and bring to a simmer. Place the casserole on the edge of the fire or prop it up with a brick or something similar – to distance it from the direct heat. (This should allow you to keep the heat low.) Simmer gently for 15 minutes or so.

4 While the tomato sauce is cooking, lay the sausages in a grill basket (fish cage) and place directly over the fire. Cook for about 4 minutes on each side until evenly coloured and cooked through, turning a few times. Take the sausages out of the basket once they are cooked.

5 Add the sausages to the casserole along with the beans. Simmer for another 10 minutes to allow the beans to soak up the flavour and heat through.

6 Just before serving, toast the slices of sourdough over the fire and butter generously. Ladle the stew into bowls and enjoy with the toast alongside.

KEEMA SPICED VENISON *on* CHAPATIS

makes **6**

Venison is an often overlooked meat, but I love its earthy flavours. It's low in fat, so it tends to dry out easily – but you want that here, as it becomes almost crispy as it cooks and takes on the aromatics from the spice mix. Cooling coriander and garlic yoghurt balances the heat.

KEEMA SPICE MIX

1 tsp coriander seeds

½ tsp black peppercorns

1 tbsp cumin seeds

½ tsp ground turmeric

½ cinnamon stick, broken up

2 cloves

3 black cardamom pods, crushed

2 bay leaves

KEEMA

3 tbsp vegetable oil or ghee

500g venison mince

1 onion, diced

4 garlic cloves, finely chopped

2cm piece of fresh ginger, finely chopped

200ml water

2 tomatoes, roughly chopped

3 long green chillies, finely sliced

100g peas

2 tbsp roughly chopped mint leaves

2 tbsp roughly chopped coriander leaves

Salt and freshly ground black pepper

CORIANDER AND GARLIC YOGHURT

150ml natural yoghurt

2 small garlic cloves, finely grated

1 tsp finely chopped coriander stalks

Ingredients continue >

1 First, prepare the spice mix. Put all of the keema spices into a dry frying pan along with the bay leaves and toast them over a medium heat on the hob for 2–3 minutes until fragrant. Remove from the heat and leave to cool, then crush to a fine powder, using a pestle and mortar or a spice grinder. Pack into a small tub until needed.

2 When you're ready to cook, place a Dutch oven or cast-iron casserole over the hot embers of your fire and add the oil or ghee. When hot, add the venison mince and cook for 10–15 minutes, stirring frequently, until well coloured and almost crispy.

3 Toss in the diced onion, stir to mix with the mince and fry for a few minutes to soften. When the onion takes on a little colour, stir in the garlic and ginger and cook for a minute or so, just to release the aromas and flavours. Now stir in 3 tbsp of the keema spice mix and cook, stirring, for 1 minute.

4 Pour in the water and bring to a simmer. Let simmer until the liquor is reduced by half; the venison will rehydrate slightly and soften.

5 Meanwhile, for the coriander and garlic yoghurt, mix the ingredients together in a small bowl and season with salt and pepper to taste; set aside.

6 Stir the chopped tomatoes, sliced chillies and peas through the keema and warm through. Season with salt and pepper to taste; keep warm. >

6 wholemeal chapatis

6 long green chillies

¼ red cabbage, cored and finely sliced

Hot sauce or tamarind sauce (optional)

Lime pickle (optional)

7 Place the chapatis on a rack over your fire to warm through for 1–2 minutes on each side. At the same time, place the whole green chillies on the rack next to the chapatis to soften, char and blister.

8 Finally, stir the herbs though the hot venison keema. To assemble, pile some shredded red cabbage onto each chapati and generously spoon on the keema mix. Add a dollop or two of the coriander and garlic yoghurt. Top with a grilled chilli, add hot sauce or tamarind sauce and/or lime pickle for extra heat if you like and tuck in!

SMORES, BAKED BANANAS *and* FRUIT KEBABS

This is perfect for getting the kids involved. My little man Acey loves the chocolate-marshmallow sandwiches and the chocolate-honeycomb baked bananas – I reckon it's a fair deal to say two fruit kebabs equals one chocolatey thing, in this three-course dessert!

· ·

SMORES

8 giant marshmallows

16 chocolate-topped biscuits (such as chocolate digestives and hob nobs)

BAKED BANANAS

4 bananas

120g chocolate honeycomb, roughly chopped

100g dark chocolate, roughly chopped

FRUIT KEBABS

600g assorted soft fruit (we used strawberries, grapes, mango and pineapple)

200ml double cream

2 tbsp honey

FOR THE SMORES skewer a giant marshmallow onto each of 8 long metal skewers and toast over the glowing embers of the fire until golden all over and starting to melt. Remove from the heat and sandwich the hot toasted marshmallow between 2 chocolate biscuits, with the chocolate on the inside. Repeat with the remaining marshmallows. Eat the smores straight away, while they're still warm and sticky.

TO PREPARE THE BANANAS peel away half of the skin along the length of each banana. Take out the banana, cut into bite-sized pieces then place back in the skin to reshape the banana. Place each one on a piece of foil (big enough to wrap it) with the exposed banana uppermost. Sprinkle with the chocolate honeycomb and dark chocolate. Bring the edges of the foil together and seal to make a parcel. Place on a grid over the glowing fire embers for 12–15 minutes to bake the bananas. You want them to be soft and squishy and for the chocolate to have created a sticky sauce.

FOR THE FRUIT KEBABS peel the fruit and cut into bite-sized pieces if necessary. Skewer onto mini skewers, alternating the different fruit. Whip the cream and honey together in a bowl until soft peaks form. Serve the mini fruit kebabs with the flavoured cream in a small bowl alongside.

Sides

SALAD
TEXTURE
SLAW

SIDES

When you're planning a barbecue menu, never let the sides be an after-thought — they are the glue that holds it all together. If you're taking the time to prepare and cook an impressive main course, you want to make sure the sides match up.

I tend to prepare at least one side for every main and I like to think about creating a good balance of tastes and textures across the menu. If you've gone big on spice with the main event, choose a cooling side to even things out, like the grilled hispi cabbage Caesar on page 208.

Or if you want something crunchy and fresh, try one of the slaws on pages 201 and 211.

Lots of these side dishes can be made in advance and the final bits added just before you're ready to serve, so you can concentrate on looking after the barbecue. The charred cauliflower salad with feta on page 197 is a great example of this — you can get the cauliflower on just 10 minutes before you want to eat. It is packed with so many amazing layers of texture and flavour: pops of sweetness from the pomegranate seeds balanced by salty feta, heat from the chillies and a bit of sharpness from preserved lemons. It's almost a meal in itself.

Sides are also an opportunity to get a bit creative and try something new – if you've never grilled a cucumber before, you're missing out! It tastes amazing with halloumi and spiced chickpeas in the salad on page 202 so give it a go next time. You don't want the sides to steal the show though, so if your main course has quite subtle flavours going on – maybe some simply grilled fish or seafood – then you'll probably want to avoid a dish with very bold spicing. The warm herby potato salad on page 205 will go with almost anything and is great for adding a bit of bulk.

Like the starters and sharing platters that kick off your barbecue, side dishes give you the opportunity to add extra flavour and to experience a whole range of exciting tastes and interesting textures.

WARM COURGETTE, FETA *and* HERB SALAD

In this versatile salad, charred courgettes – straight from the grill – are mixed with cool, creamy feta and crunchy lettuce leaves. With black olives and fresh herbs scattered through, plus a subtle chilli kick, it will complement most dishes while holding its own on the flavour front.

100g feta, crumbled

2 little gem lettuces, leaves separated

1 green pepper, cored, deseeded and diced

½ red chilli, finely sliced

½ bunch of mint, stalks removed

½ bunch of coriander, leaves picked and stalks chopped

4 medium courgettes

A little cold-pressed rapeseed oil

100g pitted black olives, roughly chopped

Salt and freshly ground black pepper

DRESSING

20ml sherry vinegar

75ml cold-pressed rapeseed oil or extra virgin olive oil

1 Put the feta, lettuce leaves, green pepper, red chilli, mint leaves and coriander leaves and stalks into a large bowl and set aside.

2 Cut the courgettes on the diagonal into 4–5mm thick slices and place in another bowl. Season with salt and pepper and trickle over a little rapeseed oil. Turn the courgettes to oil them lightly.

3 When you are ready to serve, lay the courgette slices directly on a hot barbecue grid and char on both sides, turning with tongs as necessary. Once they are ready, add them to the bowl of salad. Scatter over the black olives and toss to mix. Season with salt and pepper to taste.

4 Trickle the sherry vinegar and rapeseed or olive oil over the salad, season lightly with salt and pepper and toss gently to dress. Transfer to a salad bowl to serve.

BARBECUE-STYLE CAPONATA

Red peppers and aubergines become intensely smoky and delicious when they're cooked whole on the barbecue. For this Mediterranean side, they're combined with garlic, red onion and capers, and topped with basil and pine nuts. It works well with fish, lamb or chicken.

· ·

2 aubergines

2 large red peppers

80ml extra virgin olive oil

2 small red onions, diced

4 garlic cloves, finely sliced

6 celery sticks, sliced

400g cherry tomatoes (ideally a mix of colours), halved

2 tbsp capers

3 tbsp red wine vinegar

Salt and freshly ground black pepper

TO FINISH

2 large handfuls of basil leaves

30g pine nuts, toasted

1 Place the aubergines and red peppers on a hot barbecue and cook for around 15 minutes, turning regularly, until evenly blackened all over. The red peppers will cook faster – when they are ready, pop them into a bowl and cover with cling film. When the aubergines are softened and begin to collapse, they are ready. Place them in a separate bowl and cover with cling film.

2 Heat the olive oil in a large cast-iron frying pan over a medium heat on the barbecue. When hot, add the red onions and garlic and sauté for 3–4 minutes. Add the celery and cook for a further 2–3 minutes or until it is slightly softened. Remove the pan from the heat and leave to cool slightly.

3 Meanwhile, take the peppers from their bowl, peel away their skins and remove all the seeds. Remove the skin from the aubergines, too. Cut both the aubergines and peppers into large dice. Add these to a large salad bowl, along with the sautéed onion and celery.

4 Add the cherry tomatoes, capers and wine vinegar. Mix well and season with salt and pepper to taste. Scatter over the basil leaves and toasted pine nuts to serve.

TIP

If you have leftovers, this caponata will keep for days in the fridge and gets better the longer you leave it. Served with crusty bread to mop up the delicious juices, it makes a great lunch.

CHARRED CAULIFLOWER SALAD *with* FETA

Cauliflower is great cooked over flames, as it retains its shape and develops a subtle sweetness. This vibrant salad is packed with so many textures and layers of flavour: feta provides a sharp saltiness, and pomegranate seeds bring little bursts of sugary crunch.

2 medium cauliflowers

1 tbsp ras el hanout

1 tbsp ground turmeric

80ml rapeseed oil

3 tbsp water

2 tsp salt

100g podded broad beans, blanched and skinned

2 green chillies, sliced

200g block of feta, crumbled

30 pitted green olives

20 sun-blushed tomatoes

1 preserved lemon, finely chopped

YOGHURT DRESSING

150g natural yoghurt

1 tbsp harissa paste

Juice of ½ lemon

TO FINISH

100g pomegranate seeds

60g pine nuts, toasted

1 tbsp chopped mint

1 Slice off the stem bases of the cauliflowers, then cut each one into even-sized small florets. Lay the cauliflower florets in a tray, sprinkle with the spices and drizzle over the rapeseed oil and water. Season with the salt and mix well with your hands until evenly coated.

2 Lay the cauliflower florets directly on the hot barbecue and cook until charred and toasty on all sides, turning as necessary. This will take around 10 minutes. Return the cauliflower to the tray and leave to cool a little.

3 Meanwhile, mix the ingredients for the yoghurt dressing together in a small bowl.

4 Add the rest of the salad ingredients to the cauliflower, distributing them evenly. Drizzle the yoghurt dressing over the salad, then scatter over the pomegranate seeds, toasted pine nuts and chopped mint to serve.

BIG GREEN SALAD

serves 6

Healthy, sweet, crunchy and packed with ten varieties of veg and herbs, this versatile salad is a real celebration of all things green! It's a go-to for your barbecue menu that will work with absolutely anything in this book.

3 little gem lettuces, leaves separated

50g baby spinach leaves

50g rocket leaves

200g tenderstem broccoli, blanched

125g mangetout, trimmed

100g frozen peas, thawed

150g baby cucumbers, thickly sliced

1 ripe avocado

A handful of mint leaves, roughly chopped

A handful of parsley leaves, roughly chopped

DRESSING

4 tbsp extra virgin olive oil

1 heaped tsp Dijon mustard

2 tbsp white wine vinegar

1 tbsp maple syrup

Salt and freshly ground black pepper

TO FINISH

30g pumpkin seeds, toasted

1 Put all the salad leaves into a serving bowl. Cut the blanched broccoli and mangetout into 2.5cm pieces and add to the bowl with the peas and sliced baby cucumbers. Toss gently to mix.

2 For the dressing, put the olive oil, mustard, wine vinegar and maple syrup into a small bowl and whisk until smooth. Season with salt and pepper.

3 When you are ready to serve, halve, peel, de-stone and slice the avocado then add it to the salad. Scatter over the chopped herbs, too. Trickle the dressing over and toss to coat the salad ingredients evenly. Sprinkle with the toasted pumpkin seeds and enjoy!

COLESLAW WITH RADISH AND SPRING ONION

No barbecue is complete without a good slaw. Of course, there's
nothing wrong with buying coleslaw, but it's easy to make your own.
This version includes radishes, which give it a peppery kick that's
enhanced by the mustardy mayonnaise dressing.

1 red onion

1 Spanish onion

10 radishes, thinly sliced

¼ white cabbage, tough core removed

A bunch of spring onions, finely sliced

DRESSING

80g mayonnaise

1 tbsp English mustard

1 tsp cracked black pepper

A good pinch of salt

1 Slice the red and Spanish onions very finely and place
in a large salad bowl with the sliced radishes. Shred the
white cabbage finely and add to the bowl.

2 For the dressing, in a small bowl, mix together the
mayonnaise, mustard, cracked pepper and salt.

3 Add the dressing to the cabbage mix and toss well to
coat everything evenly. Scatter over the spring onions,
toss again and your coleslaw is ready to serve.

CUCUMBER, HALLOUMI *and* SPICED CHICKPEAS

serves 4

Cooking cucumbers on the barbecue might sound a bit weird, but trust me – the taste is amazing! They char up beautifully and the seeds take on a really great toasted flavour, which goes well with spicy chickpeas and salty halloumi.

3 cucumbers

2 tsp flaky sea salt

About 3 tbsp rapeseed oil

2 x 225g packs halloumi, each cut into 6 slices

Juice of 1 lime

1 tsp dried chilli flakes

¼ bunch of coriander, roughly chopped

¼ bunch of flat-leaf parsley, roughly chopped

3 pickled green chillies, sliced

Salt and freshly ground black pepper

SPICED CHICKPEAS

400g tin chickpeas, drained and rinsed

3 tbsp rapeseed oil

½ tsp dried herbes de Provence

½ tsp cayenne pepper

¼ tsp ground cumin

TO SERVE

2 limes, cut into wedges

1 Peel the cucumbers, halve them lengthways and lay flat side up on a tray. Sprinkle over the 2 tsp flaky salt and leave for an hour or so, to draw out the moisture.

2 While the cucumber is salting, tip the chickpeas into a bowl and add the rapeseed oil, dried herbs, spices and some salt and pepper. Stir well, then spread the chickpeas out evenly on a large, sturdy baking tray. Place under a low grill to toast and crisp up – this will take a good 30 minutes. Once toasty and golden, remove from the grill and leave to cool.

3 When you are ready to cook the cucumbers, pat dry with kitchen paper and place on a clean, dry tray. Drizzle with a little rapeseed oil.

4 Now place the cucumber flat side down on your hot barbecue along with the halloumi slices and cook for 3–4 minutes. Turn the cucumber and halloumi slices over and cook for another 2 minutes, then remove from the heat and lay on a tray. Trickle over the lime juice and sprinkle with the chilli flakes.

5 Chop the warm cucumber and halloumi into bite-sized pieces and place in a serving bowl. Add a little more rapeseed oil, the chopped fresh herbs and pickled chilli slices. Toss together and season with salt and pepper to taste. Serve with lime wedges, for an extra hit of citrus.

WARM HERBY NEW POTATO SALAD

This simple recipe uses ingredients we are all familiar with, but cooking the potatoes over the barbecue introduces a fantastic smokiness that you can't achieve in the kitchen. Dressing the salad while the potatoes are still warm means they'll absorb all the delicious herby flavours.

800g new potatoes, boiled until just tender, drained and halved

4 garlic cloves (skin on), bashed

3 rosemary sprigs, leaves picked and roughly torn

2 tbsp good-quality olive oil

Salt and freshly ground black pepper

CHIVE DRESSING

1 tbsp English mustard

1 tbsp runny honey

2 tbsp chopped chives

2 tbsp good-quality olive oil

1 Put the boiled new potatoes, bashed garlic cloves and rosemary in a large sturdy baking tray. Season well with salt and pepper, trickle over the olive oil and toss together.

2 Place the tray of potatoes on the hot barbecue. Cook for 3 minutes and then give the potatoes a good shake. Cook them for a further 3 minutes until hot through. Remove from the barbecue and leave until cool enough to handle.

3 Meanwhile, for the chive dressing, whisk the ingredients together in a small bowl.

4 Pick out the rosemary sprigs from the tray. Trickle the dressing over the hot potatoes, toss well to coat and leave to stand and soak up the flavour for 5 minutes or so. Taste to check the seasoning and serve while still warm.

BARBECUED GREEN BEANS *and* ASPARAGUS

serves 6

I love asparagus and beans barbecued very simply – but this warm Asian-inspired dish is all about the sweet sesame and maple dressing. Feel free to play around with the veg: purple sprouting broccoli, sugar snaps, anything you can grill that will retain a nice crunch works well.

500g asparagus spears

500g green beans, tops trimmed

2 tbsp soy sauce (Kikkoman)

3 tbsp vegetable oil

DRESSING

2 tbsp tahini

1 tbsp soy sauce (Kikkoman)

1cm thick slice of fresh ginger, finely grated

1 tbsp maple syrup

2 tbsp rice vinegar

1 tsp sesame oil

TO FINISH

2 tbsp toasted sesame seeds

1 To prepare the asparagus, bend each spear near the base until it snaps naturally, and discard the woody end bit. Lay the asparagus spears in a shallow tray. Place the green beans in a separate tray.

2 Add half the soy sauce and half the vegetable oil to each tray and toss both the beans and asparagus well until evenly coated.

3 For the dressing, put all the ingredients into a small bowl and whisk together until smooth.

4 Lay the asparagus on the hot barbecue, in lines across the grid. Cook for 1–2 minutes on each side or until lightly charred and cooked through. Lift the asparagus spears off the barbecue and place them back on the tray. Barbecue the green beans in the same way and add them to the asparagus.

5 Mix the asparagus and beans together and transfer to a large shallow serving dish. Drizzle over the dressing and sprinkle with the toasted sesame seeds to serve.

GRILLED HISPI CABBAGE CAESAR

In this barbecue twist on an American classic, the creamy, cheesy anchovy dressing sits perfectly on the sweet charred cabbage and crisp sourdough croûtons. If you're unsure about barbecuing cabbage, I urge you to give it a go – the smoke gives it an incredible flavour.

· ·

2 hispi cabbage (or sweetheart/ pointy cabbages)

2 tbsp olive oil

Flaky salt

SOURDOUGH CROÛTONS

150g sourdough, torn into bite-sized pieces

40g butter, melted

2 tbsp olive oil

1 garlic clove, finely grated

A pinch of salt

1 tbsp finely chopped flat-leaf parsley

CHEAT'S CAESAR DRESSING

200g mayonnaise

A pinch of salt

20g Dijon mustard

3 good-quality salted anchovies (Ortiz), chopped

3 garlic cloves, grated

60g Parmesan, finely grated

Juice of 1 lemon

¼ tsp cracked black pepper

1–2 tbsp milk (optional)

TO FINISH

8 good-quality salted anchovies (Ortiz)

20g Parmesan

1 First, prepare the sourdough croûtons. In a bowl, toss the sourdough pieces with the melted butter, olive oil and garlic to coat all over. Spread them out on a sturdy baking tray and toast under a medium-hot grill for 10–15 minutes, turning them as necessary to ensure they colour evenly.

2 When ready to cook, cut each cabbage vertically into quarters, through the base, so you have 8 wedges. Drizzle the cabbage lightly with olive oil and sprinkle with a little flaky salt.

3 Place the cabbage halves flat side down on the hot barbecue and cook for 8 minutes or so, until charred and crispy. Flip the halves over and spray with some water. Now cover loosely with foil so that the cabbage steams slightly over the heat for a few minutes, or until it is just cooked – you want it to have a bit of bite.

4 Meanwhile, for the dressing, put all the ingredients into a small bowl and mix together well, adding a little milk to loosen the dressing if needed.

5 Once cooked, remove the cabbage portions from the barbecue and transfer them to a warmed serving dish. Drizzle the dressing all over the cabbage, then scatter over the sourdough croûtons and anchovies. Finally, shave or grate over the Parmesan and serve.

SPICY FENNEL *and* POMEGRANATE SLAW

As a variation on classic slaw, this is a lovely spicy one that goes well with Middle Eastern-style dishes, such as the koftas on page 81. Using fennel as well as white cabbage introduces a great aniseed taste, and yoghurt instead of mayonnaise gives it a lighter consistency.

1 large fennel bulb, core removed

¼ white cabbage, tough core removed

1 onion, thinly sliced

2 green chillies, finely sliced

Juice of 1 lime

DRESSING

4 tbsp Greek yoghurt

3 tbsp water

½ tsp ground turmeric

Salt and freshly ground black pepper

TO FINISH

A handful of mint leaves

100g pomegranate seeds

1 Shred the fennel and white cabbage finely. Place in a large bowl with the onion, green chillies and lime juice and toss to combine.

2 For the dressing, mix the yoghurt, water and turmeric together in a small bowl until smoothly combined. Season with salt and pepper to taste.

3 Add the dressing to the fennel mix and toss well to coat everything. Scatter over the torn mint and pomegranate seeds, toss again and the slaw is ready to go.

FENNEL AND CABBAGE SLAW

This is a lovely variation for a less spicy slaw. Omit the green chillies, pomegranate seeds and mint. Use a medium fennel bulb and add ¼ red cabbage, finely shredded, and 1 carrot, grated. For the dressing, mix 6 tbsp thick mayonnaise with 2 tbsp white wine vinegar, 2 tbsp American mustard, a handful of coriander leaves, roughly chopped, and some salt and pepper. Add to the veg and toss to combine, then serve.

GREEK SALAD

You can't go wrong with a Greek salad, it's always a crowd-pleaser. Get yourself some great ingredients and let them do the hard work for you. A good-quality olive oil will make all the difference here. Serve this with chicken or lamb for a Mediterranean feast.

1 small red pepper

1 small green pepper

1 red onion, diced

4 celery sticks, thickly sliced

6 baby cucumbers, thickly sliced

250g cherry tomatoes (ideally a mix of colours), halved

120g Kalamata olives

4 tbsp extra virgin olive oil

1 tbsp red wine vinegar

Juice of 1 lemon

1 tsp dried oregano

2 x 200g blocks of feta

Salt and freshly ground black pepper

1 Halve, core and deseed the peppers then cut into 2.5cm dice. Place in a large bowl with the red onion, celery, cucumber, tomatoes and olives.

2 Add 3 tbsp of the olive oil, along with the wine vinegar, lemon juice and ½ tsp dried oregano. Season liberally with salt and pepper and mix well. Leave to marinate for 10 minutes or so.

3 Transfer the salad to a large shallow bowl. Place the two blocks of feta on top of the salad and drizzle over the rest of the olive oil. Sprinkle with the remaining ½ tsp dried oregano and serve.

TIP

Using big blocks of feta makes it easier for people to take as big a piece as they want.

Desserts + Drinks

SWEET FRUITY TREATS

DESSERTS & DRINKS

When you really don't want the celebrations to end, a barbecued dessert can extend the fun a bit longer. Yes, you could just have some ice cream from the freezer, but it's so easy to grill a bit of fruit or toast a few brioche slices.

Brioche and other cakey styles of bread toast up perfectly and they'll absorb all those remaining great smoky flavours. Grilling fruit caramelises their natural sugars beautifully, producing an irresistible bitter-sweet flavour that's like the top of a crème brûlée. You can barbecue almost any variety, but chunky fruits – like pineapple, mango and stone fruits – will hold their shape best. Or you could always set a pan on top of the barbecue and warm up a few soft fruits and berries to spoon over brioche or serve alongside ice cream.

The barbecued sliced watermelon on page 226 might sound a bit unusual, but the outer layers char up brilliantly and it becomes lovely and warm – perfect next to the cooling crunch of the accompanying granita.

As with most things, it's all in the detail, and welcoming your guests with a specially made drink will immediately get everyone in the party mood. For a taste of Mexico, try the mezcal cooler made with pear, grapefruit and deliciously citrusy yuzu on page 231. The pale ale cocktail on the same page packs a bit of a punch while being the perfect refreshing summertime drink.

Or for a really fruity thirst-quencher, make up a big batch of the kombucha spritz on page 230. Also have a few jugs of soft drinks and iced water around – you can add flavour to the water with fresh mint and lemon or lime slices to keep it interesting.

When you want to impress and make sure everyone has a good time, it's these little extras that will make your barbecue all the more memorable.

CHARRED PINEAPPLE *with* SALTED RUM CARAMEL

serves 4

Pineapple is a great ingredient on the barbecue because it holds its shape and is packed with natural sugars, so it caramelises all over. Lime zest, rum and a pinch of salt stop it from being overly sweet, while coconut flakes and pecans provide a satisfying crunch.

1 medium super-sweet pineapple
A little olive oil to brush

NUT BROWN BUTTER

80g butter
Finely grated zest and juice of 1 lime

SALTED RUM CARAMEL SAUCE

130g dark muscovado sugar
30g butter
30ml dark rum
150ml double cream
A pinch of flaky salt

TO SERVE

A handful of toasted coconut flakes
A handful of pecan nuts, toasted
4 scoops of coconut ice cream

1 To prepare the pineapple, stand it upright on a board and slice off the peel, removing the 'eyes'; leave the leafy tops attached. Quarter the pineapple lengthways into 4 long wedges.

2 For the nut brown butter, heat the butter in a small cast-iron saucepan on the barbecue until it starts to turn nutty brown. Take off the heat and add the lime juice to stop the cooking and add flavour. Allow to cool a little, then stir in the lime zest and set aside for later.

3 Brush the pineapple wedges with a little olive oil and lay them on the barbecue with the leaves overhanging the edge of the grid so they don't burn; this will also make it easier to turn them. Cook for about 12 minutes, turning the pineapple every 2–3 minutes and brushing it with the nut brown butter frequently; this will help it to caramelise as it cooks.

4 Meanwhile, for the salted rum caramel sauce, put all the ingredients into a small cast-iron pan on the barbecue. Bring to a simmer, stirring, and cook gently for about 5 minutes or until lightly thickened.

5 Once the pineapple is nicely caramelised, lift it off the barbecue and place in a large bowl. Let it rest for 5 minutes, then scatter over the coconut flakes and pecans.

6 To serve, place a portion of pineapple on each plate, pour on some caramel sauce and add a scoop of coconut ice cream.

CHARRED MANGO, STICKY RICE *and* THAI BASIL SYRUP

In this spin on rice pudding, the rice is cooked in coconut milk and served with a sticky honey and basil syrup. Mangoes are high in sugar so they char really well – just make sure your mango is a little bit firm because if it's too ripe, it will stick to the grill!

4 ripe mangoes

STICKY RICE

200g jasmine rice

400ml tin coconut milk

150ml water

50g palm sugar, grated

A pinch of salt

THAI BASIL SYRUP

100ml water

5 tbsp honey

Grated zest of 1 lime

Juice of 2 limes

6 Thai basil sprigs, roughly chopped, plus extra leaves to finish

1 For the sticky rice, put all the ingredients into a small non-stick saucepan and bring to a gentle simmer over a medium heat on the hob. Stir the rice and reduce the heat to a very low simmer. Put the lid on the pan and leave to cook for 25 minutes or until all the liquid is absorbed.

2 For the Thai basil syrup, put all the ingredients into a small sauté pan and bring to a simmer over a medium-high heat. Continue to simmer until the mixture thickens to a syrup consistency. Pour the syrup through a sieve into a small jug or bowl and set aside.

3 Cut the cheeks from each mango, either side of the stone, and score the flesh in a criss-cross pattern. (Feel free to devour the rest of the mango!) Place the mango cheeks, flesh side down, on a hot barbecue for 3–4 minutes or until the flesh is charred and softened.

4 Place a couple of barbecued mango cheeks on each warmed plate, add a big spoonful of warm sticky rice and drizzle with a little of the syrup. Finish with a Thai basil leaf and serve.

BRIOCHE EGGY BREAD *with* BOOZY APRICOTS

serves 4

Here is a proper indulgent dessert — if you have a sweet tooth this one is for you! The eggy bread has a slight crunch, which is delicious with soft, sticky apricots and boozy caramel sauce. Keep a close eye on the brioche, as it has a high sugar content and will burn quite easily.

BRIOCHE EGGY BREAD

3 large free-range eggs

75ml double cream

½ tsp ground cinnamon

4 thick slices of brioche (4cm thick)

BOOZY APRICOTS

8 apricots, halved and de-stoned

100g butter

80g soft light brown sugar

50ml double cream

50ml Marsala

TO SERVE

200ml double cream, lightly whipped

1 For the eggy bread, crack the eggs into a shallow bowl. Add the cream and cinnamon and beat well with a fork to combine. Dip each slice of brioche into the egg mixture very briefly to coat, then place on a tray and bring it over to the barbecue.

2 Lay the apricot halves cut side down directly on the hot barbecue. Cook for a minute or two on each side until you have char marks on both sides. Remove to a plate, while the apricots are still holding their shape.

3 For the boozy caramel sauce, put the butter, sugar, cream and Marsala into a small cast-iron saucepan and place on the barbecue over a low to medium heat. Stir until the sugar is dissolved and the mixture is bubbling.

4 You want to cook the brioche once the embers have cooled down a bit — on the edges of the barbecue to achieve a medium to low heat. Lightly oil the grid to avoid sticking, then add the eggy brioche slices. Cook, turning every minute or so, for about 5 minutes until you get a lovely brown crust on both sides.

5 Place a slice of eggy brioche on each plate. Add the apricots and spoon on the boozy caramel sauce. Add a big dollop of whipped cream, trickle over any remaining sauce and eat immediately.

BARBECUED NECTARINES *with* VANILLA CREAM

Barbecued nectarines are delicious, especially when you serve them alongside cream that's been infused with vanilla and lemon zest. This simple trick brings restaurant-standard sophistication to an easy dessert. Raspberries provide a touch of sharpness.

4 ripe nectarines
2 tbsp rapeseed oil
4 tbsp caster sugar

VANILLA CREAM

200ml double cream
1 vanilla pod, split
Finely grated zest of 1 lemon
2–3 tbsp icing sugar

TO SERVE

80g raspberries
4 shortbread biscuits

1 Halve and de-stone the nectarines. Brush the cut surface of each nectarine half with a little rapeseed oil. Place flat side down on a hot barbecue for 30 seconds – 1 minute or until you get a lovely light char on the underside. Remove from the barbecue and place the nectarines, flat side up, on a metal tray; set aside to cool slightly.

2 Meanwhile, for the vanilla cream, pour the cream into a bowl. Scrape the seeds from the vanilla pod, using the tip of a knife, and add them to the cream with the lemon zest and icing sugar to taste. Whip until the cream thickens enough to form soft peaks.

3 Sprinkle a light, even layer of caster sugar on the cut side of each nectarine half and run a cook's blowtorch over the surface to caramelise the sugar. To warm the nectarines slightly if necessary, place them on the edge of the barbecue.

4 To serve, place two nectarine halves on each plate and add a large dollop of vanilla cream and some raspberries. Serve with the shortbread biscuits.

BARBECUED WATERMELON *and* RASPBERRY GRANITA

The combination of hot watermelon and icy, sweet and tangy granita may sound unusual, but I promise it tastes amazing. This dessert works almost like a palate cleanser – perfect after you've indulged in a couple of burgers or hot dogs!

6 thick slices of watermelon
(200g each)

RASPBERRY GRANITA

300ml water

150g golden caster sugar

A large handful of mint leaves, roughly chopped, plus extra sprigs to finish

Grated zest of 1 lime

Juice of 2 limes

300g raspberries

Mint sprigs to finish

1 Make the granita several hours ahead. Pour the water into a small pan and add the sugar, chopped mint, lime zest and lime juice. Place over a medium-high heat and stir until the sugar is dissolved. Remove from the heat and strain the liquor into a bowl to remove the mint. Add the raspberries to the lime syrup and leave to cool slightly.

2 Tip the raspberries and lime syrup into a jug blender and blitz until smooth. Pour the mixture through a sieve into a small shallow container, to remove the raspberry seeds. Place in the freezer for 1–2 hours until the mixture starts to freeze around the edges.

3 Using a fork, scrape the partially frozen granita towards the centre of the container. Repeat every 30 minutes until the mixture is completely frozen.

4 When you're ready to serve, lay the watermelon slices on your hot barbecue and cook for 1–2 minutes on each side or until lightly charred.

5 Transfer the barbecued watermelon to serving plates. Spoon the granita into glasses, top each serving with a mint sprig and serve alongside. Hot watermelon and cold granita – a great combo!

KOMBUCHA SPRITZ,
MEZCAL COOLER *and*
FRUITY PALE ALE COCKTAIL

KOMBUCHA SPRITZ

Kombucha has really taken off here in recent years. It has a lovely fermented flavour with a slight fizz, and comes in different flavours. It's great paired with ginger beer in this refreshing drink! You can mix things up with different types of kombucha and fresh fruit.

400ml raspberry kombucha

200ml ginger beer

100ml pomegranate juice

100g mixed berries, such as raspberries, blueberries and strawberries

A handful of mint leaves, roughly torn

Ice cubes to serve

1 Pour the raspberry kombucha, ginger beer and pomegranate juice into a large jug. Slice or quarter any larger fruit, such as strawberries, then add all the berries to the jug.

2 Stir well with a long spoon. Add the torn mint and plenty of ice cubes to the jug and mix again.

3 Pour the kombucha spritz into glasses and make sure everyone gets a few mixed berries and mint to enjoy.

KOMBUCHA COCKTAIL

Feel free to add a generous splash of vodka or gin to the spritz for a boozy summer cocktail!

MEZCAL COOLER

In this cocktail, pear juice softens the flavours of punchy mezcal, sweet agave, and citrusy yuzu and grapefruit. This is the perfect drink for a summer day. It is also wonderfully refreshing as a non-alcoholic drink if you leave out the mezcal.

150ml mezcal

Juice of 2 large pink grapefruit (350ml)

150ml pear juice

2 tbsp agave

20ml yuzu juice

Ice cubes to serve

Slices of pink grapefruit to finish

1 Pour the mezcal, grapefruit juice, pear juice, agave and yuzu juice into a large jug and mix well with a spoon. Fill the jug with ice and mix again.

2 Pour the cocktail into glasses and add a slice of pink grapefruit to each one.

FRUITY PALE ALE COCKTAIL

American pale ales have a lovely hoppy, almost herbal flavour that's enhanced by the basil in this fruity rum cocktail. Combined with the subtle bitterness of Campari and a bit of sweet mango purée, it makes the perfect drink for those long barbecue afternoons.

12 basil leaves

200ml white rum

120ml mango purée

400ml American pale ale

60ml Campari

Loads of crushed ice to serve

1 Place 3 basil leaves in each of 4 glasses and bruise the leaves with the thin end of a wooden spoon.

2 Three-quarters fill each glass with crushed ice. Pour in the white rum, mango purée and pale ale, then stir with a cocktail stirrer to mix.

3 To serve, top up each glass with the Campari. Add straws and sip away.

INDEX

Thanks!

Here comes a massive list of thank you's to everybody who has been involved in creating this book – everyone on these pages has worked absolute magic to get the words and pictures onto bits of paper. What we have managed to create in such a short space of time is heroic! I've always been a big fan of no-stress cooking and now I'm a fan of not overthinking books too, because this has been about taking things back to basics, starting a fire of imagination and cooking to create something magical for everyone to enjoy. To the whole team at Bloomsbury and Absolute, you guys have pulled out all the stops: Jon Croft, Rowan Yapp, Xa Shaw Stewart, Ellen Williams, Donough Shanahan and Laura Brodie – top work.

I'd like to thank the designers at Superfantastic for creating a super set of pages that I am very proud of: Mark Arn and Gillian Campbell, you've done a great job. Big thanks also to Jim Smith for rolling out the fantastic design.

I value a cookery book for its visuals and the simplicity of its recipe text, but none of it works without beautiful words that are easy to understand. That skill is showcased so well here by Laura Bayliss, with great editing by Janet Illsley.

As always, the ever-important pictures have been taken by my great friend and magician-with-a-camera, Cristian Barnett. A huge thank you to Cristian and Lisa Paige-Smith for making the photographs beautiful, arty, inviting, vibrant and fun. Obviously, for the visuals to look good, the styling and art direction has to be on point. So, thank you to Lydia McPherson and Lauren Miller for your eyes on setting everything up.

A huge shout out to the food team who put everything together for Cristian's photography: Nicole Herft, Chris Mackett, Rosie Mackean, Simone Shagam and Holly Cochrane. You guys work so hard cooking and creating. Special thanks to Nicole and Chris, not only for making the food look great and taste great, but also for their recipe development. They find exciting flavours from around the world with Nicole's food knowledge, and develop dishes that sit so comfortably with me – thanks Chris. None of this would be possible without your dedication and brilliant efforts.

From the book team to 'Team Life', a massive shout out to everybody who helps create the bigger picture: Emma Harrand, Alan Dooley, Warren Geraghty and the whole of the Hand and Flowers crew. By that, I mean everyone who works in the pubs, restaurants and festivals.

A huge thank you to Borra Garson at DML for constantly building bridges and setting everything up. A big shout out to Bone Soup and the team at the television production company for helping to create moving images. And lastly a massive thank you to Heidi Johnson-Cash and her team at Brand Pilot for the focus on brand-building Team Tom.

BLOOMSBURY ABSOLUTE
Bloomsbury Publishing Plc
50 Bedford Square, London, WC1B 3DP, UK
29 Earlsfort Terrace, Dublin 2, Ireland

BLOOMSBURY, BLOOMSBURY ABSOLUTE, the Diana logo and
the Absolute Press logo are trademarks of Bloomsbury Publishing Plc

First published in Great Britain 2021

A catalogue record for this book is available from the British Library

ISBN: HB: 978-1-5266-4142-7; Signed HB: 978-1-4729-9263-5; eBook: 978-1-5266-4140-3

10 9 8 7 6 5 4 3 2 1

PROJECT EDITOR: Janet Illsley
COVER, ILLUSTRATIONS AND TYPOGRAPHY: Superfantastic
LAYOUT DESIGN: Jim Smith
PHOTOGRAPHY: Cristian Barnett
FOOD STYLING: Nicole Herft and Chris Mackett
PROP STYLING: Lydia McPherson
INDEXER: Hilary Bird

Thanks to the following for contributing barbecues and equipment for the photography:
Big Green Egg & OFYR at Alfresco concepts (thanks to David, James, Ben, Sal and Alex): www.biggreenegg.co.uk.
The team at Weber (Giles and Dan): www.weber.com/GB/en/home
Caroline at Bar-Be-Quick: barbequick.com/grillguide
Zak at Kin Boards for the stunning boards: kinwoodboards.co.uk
Gav Monery at MoneryKnives: Instagram @monerycustomcutlery

Printed and bound in Germany by Mohn Media

To find out more about our authors and books visit www.bloomsbury.com and sign up for our newsletters